JOURNAL COLLECTION
YEARS 1995 TO 2000

Taking the Stress Out of Raising Great Kids

Jim Fay, Charles Fay, Ph.D.
& Foster W. Cline, M.D.

Love and Logic®
INSTITUTE, Inc.

The Love and Logic Institute, Inc.
2207 Jackson Street
Golden, Colorado 80401-2300
www.loveandlogic.com

Institute For Professional Development, Ltd. d.b.a. The Love and Logic Institute, Inc.
2207 Jackson Street, Golden, CO 80401-2300
www.loveandlogic.com
800-338-4065

Library of Congress Cataloging-in-Publication Data

Fay, Jim.
  Taking the stress out of raising great kids : Love and logic journal collection years 1995 to 2000 / Jim Fay, Charles Fay, and Foster W. Cline.
     p. cm.
  1. Child rearing. 2. Parenting. I. Fay, Charles, 1964- II. Cline, Foster. III. Title.
HQ769.F2327 2005
649'.1--dc22

                                         2005018602

Project Coordinator: Carol Thomas
Editing by Jason Cook, Denver, CO
Indexing by Dianne J. Nelson, Shadow Canyon Graphics, Golden, CO
Cover and interior design by Michael Snell
     Shade of the Cottonwood, Topeka, KS

Published and Printed in the United States of America

CONTENTS

JIM FAY

The legendary Jim Fay began his career as a teacher and for over three decades served in public, private, and parochial schools. He spent seventeen years as a school principal and administrator, and for nearly thirty years has been a public speaker. Jim has served as a national and international educational consultant to schools, parent organizations, counselors, mental health organizations, and the U.S. military.

Jim believes his major accomplishment in life is the development of a unique philosophy of practical techniques for enhancing communication between children and adults, known as Love and Logic. Jim has taken complex problems and broken them down into simple, easy-to-use concepts and techniques that can be understood and used by anyone. Hundreds of thousands of people have expressed how Love and Logic has enhanced their relationships with their children.

Jim is one of America's most sought after presenters in the area of parenting and school discipline. His practical techniques are revolutionizing the way parents and professionals deal with children to help them become responsible, thinking people and enhance their own self-concept.

CHARLES FAY, PH.D.

Charles Fay, Ph.D., is a parent, school psychologist, author, and consultant to schools, parent groups, and mental health professionals across the United States. His expertise in developing and teaching practical discipline strategies has been refined through work with severely disturbed youth in school, hospital, and community settings. Charles has assisted many thousands of parents and teachers in learning practical and powerful techniques to gain control of their homes and classrooms, maintain loving relationships with their children, and prepare children to become responsible and caring adults. His book *Love and Logic Magic for Early Childhood: Practical Parenting from Birth to Six Years* has obtained bestseller status. Charles frequently comments, "After all of these years, I still love being around my dad!"

FOSTER W. CLINE, M.D.

Dr. Cline is a nationally recognized psychiatrist and cofounder of the Cline/Fay Institute, Inc. He is a favorite consultant to psychiatric institutes, schools, and parent groups. His writings are the source of many revolutionary approaches to dealing with childhood problems. He has written several books, including *Uncontrollable Kids: From Heartbreak to Hope* and, coauthoring with Jim Fay, *Parenting with Love and Logic, Parenting Teens with Love and Logic,* and *Grandparenting with Love and Logic.*

Foster is known for his ability to provide creative, effective solutions for behavior problems. His presentations are lively and humorous, while providing practical techniques that produce immediate results. Foster has an uncanny ability to share his ideas and expertise in such a way that readers and audiences immediately envision themselves being more successful with young people.

The Love and Logic quarterly newsletter, known as the *Love and Logic Journal*, was first published in 1984. It was with considerable trepidation that I agreed to write the articles for the first year. I remember saying, "Once we start this, Foster and I will be obligated to come up with new topics and articles each year. I'm going to run out of material and knowledge in a short time. I can't imagine being productive and creative for more than just a few years."

What do you know? That was twenty-one years ago. The world of parenting, teaching, and childhood has continued to evolve along with all the associated new challenges and topics for articles. My worst fears didn't come true after all. Each year, people ask us for more creative solutions to new and different dilemmas.

During its first ten years the Love and Logic Institute was deluged with requests for reprints of *Journal* articles. The obvious solution to this was to publish a collection of all the articles that appeared in the *Journal*. That book was titled the *Tenth Anniversary Journal Collection*. Now that I think back on it, the title was less than creative. However, parents and teachers found great value in keeping this collection of articles close at hand as a resource for times when they experienced problems with their kids.

Ten years ago, my son, Dr. Charles Fay, joined our organization. Being a gifted writer, he contributed to the *Journal* on a regular basis—the result being that now, after another ten years, the number of articles has grown considerably larger. Because even a selection of these articles won't fit into one book, we're offering this new collection in two volumes, *Taking the Stress Out of Raising Great Kids* (years 1995 to 2000) and *More Ideas About Parenting with Less Stress* (years 2000 to 2005).

As with the first, tenth-anniversary collection, these articles are best read randomly, one at a time, as the need arises. Keep your collection in a handy place, such as on the night stand or in the bathroom, and don't be afraid to let your kids read the articles if they become curious about the development of your new skills.

The wonderful thing about Love and Logic is that even if your kids know what you are going to do, they can't stop you from doing what is right.

I hope you find this two-volume collection helpful and entertaining. Foster, Charles, and I are proud to offer our view of the world of raising and developing responsible kids who are endowed with the character to become our future leaders.

Read and enjoy,
Jim Fay, President, Love and Logic Institute, Inc.

VOLUME

11

"I Can't Protect You"
By Jim Fay
VOL. 11, NO. 1

What would you do if you found a plastic bag of marijuana in your son's room? A mother recently related this story to me.

She first wanted me to know she was not spying on her youngster, nor was she searching his room. She stumbled onto the stash of marijuana by accident. "I was so shocked," she said. "I just didn't know what to do. My day was ruined. I was depressed beyond anything I can explain."

She knew she needed to confront the issue, but just didn't know what to do or say. Since she had removed the drugs from his room, she knew she either had to put them back in the same place or talk to him soon, since he would know they had been discovered.

Her inclination was to return the bag to its original place so she could have some time to talk to someone who could give her advice. However, before Mom could act, her son returned to the house and walked in on her while she had the bag in her hand.

Needless to say, they were both shocked. There she stood in the kitchen with drugs in her hand. Her son, Mark, looked at her with eyes as big as saucers. He stuttered out something that sounded like, "It's not what you think, Mom. That's not my grass. I'm just holding it for a friend."

Mom managed to respond with, "I've heard that one before, and it doesn't matter. Drugs are not allowed in this house! I'm going to have to do something about this!"

"What, Mom?"

"I don't have the slightest idea. This is such a disappointment. This is so serious. I'm just going to have to think about this for a while. Take this bag and do something with it. I'm so upset I have to go to my room. I'll talk to you another time."

Mom agonized over this problem for the rest of the day, talked with some of her friends, and actually called one of the counselors at the high school. At the end of this time she still didn't know what to do. She just became more and more depressed about the situation.

Mark came to the dinner table, but he could not look at his mom. There was silence throughout the entire meal. When the meal was over, Mark offered to do the dishes. Mom realized this was a little unusual. He usually took off to escape to his computer. "I think he was trying to do a little damage control and soften me up," she said.

While he worked with the dishes he asked again, "You haven't told me what you're going to do about that problem. What's going on?"

Mom's response was, "I've thought of nothing else since I found your stash but I don't have any idea what to do. It's been horribly upsetting to me. I have to tell you that I'm so unhappy I can't even put it into words."

She continued with, "The thing that saddens me the most is that I know at your age I can no longer protect you from your bad decisions. I can't stand between your bad decisions and what the world has to offer for those decisions. So I guess your bad decisions are just going to have to be your bad decisions and the consequences for those decisions will have to be your consequences. You are the one who will have to deal with them and my heart will ache for you."

She went on to tell him she wasn't going to do anything about the marijuana other than to tell him it could never be in her house.

Mom went to her room a very sad person. She couldn't go to sleep so she got up and went into the living room to try to read. Before long Mark came to her with the bag of marijuana.

"Mom, I'm going to bury this stuff in the backyard."

"Why? I told you I was not going to punish you."

"Mom, you really scared me. When you told me you could no longer stand between my bad decisions and what the consequences might be, that really scared me. If you're not going to worry about that, I decided I'm going to have to."

It's wonderful to see a mother and her son learning one of the great truths about life. People tend not to worry about things when others will do their worrying for them. Children whose parents worry and remind them constantly about getting up, dressing, and getting to the school bus on time find themselves doing it constantly. The kids let them take over responsibility.

Parents who tell kids it is their responsibility to set their own alarm clocks and get themselves to the bus on time have kids who say to themselves, "If Mom isn't going to worry about this, someone better!"

Some of the best advice we have ever given parents is based upon this concept. Back out of taking over your children's responsibilities. This will teach them to think for themselves, become responsible, and be better prepared for the real world. This approach will give you time to think up some creative ways of allowing the natural consequences to fall.

© 1995 Jim Fay

Jim Fay Answers Your Questions

Vol. 11, No. 1

Question

Our community is in an uproar. We have two factions pitted against each other and the school. Each side presents good arguments. The fight is over whether our school should use "outcome-based education" or "back to the basics." Please write. What is your opinion?

Jim's Response

As to my opinion of outcome-based education, there are many different ways that it is being used. Some schools are using it effectively and focusing upon specific academic skills and learning skills. Others are using it with a focus upon issues that are difficult, if not impossible, to measure.

The issue of which is right pits groups of people against each other and causes great community arguments about the delivery of instruction.

Unfortunately, many of these educational innovations don't address the major problems the schools face. These programs are Band-Aids attempted by sincere educators to address the problem of the high number of children in classrooms who are unwilling to become involved in their own education. Educators are experiencing increasing numbers of children who are just not willing to put forth the effort needed to succeed in school.

The issue of which approach we use to deliver instruction is really not the question we should be asking. Kids thrive in almost any kind of educational setting, regardless of the way it's organized, when they come from solid families. I am talking about the kind of families where the kids are held accountable for their decisions, the kids uphold their fair share of the family work, value is placed upon struggle and effort, and parents send consistent messages about the value of education.

When kids live in families in which these attributes don't exist, the kids have trouble achieving regardless of the instruction approach taken.

Encourage your friends to spend less time worrying about the mode of instruction and more time learning how to create the responsible child who believes struggle has value. Then encourage the school to help teachers learn to work with kids in ways that cause the kids to like the teachers.

When these things happen adults will not have to worry about the education their children give themselves.

I would encourage you to listen to the audio *Shaping Self-Concept*, available in the *Love and Logic Catalog*. You will get a wealth of information about learning and motivation.

© 1995 Jim Fay

CLINE'S CORNER

On Early Abuse to Mammals: Children + Elephants
By Foster W. Cline, M.D.

VOL. 11, NO. 1

Early abuse takes an awful toll. And the problem is, the awful results don't show up for years. We all, deep down, know it. When a young human being is abused, the individual grows up to have a very difficult and angry adulthood.

New evidence shows that this appears to be true for *all* mammals. If little puppies are abused, the dogs are ruined. If horses are abused as foals, they cannot be ridden safely later. Even when elephants are abused, they do not grow up and behave normally (*Chicago Tribune*, October 2, 1994, p. 19).

This was discovered in 1994 when someone, or something, was systematically killing the beautiful white rhinos in the African Planesberg Game Reserve. The South African officials found that the rhinos had gaping wounds shaped like elephant tusks on their backs. Surprising evidence showed that young bull elephants were responsible for this unusual behavior.

The only previously recorded incidence of elephants killing rhinos had occurred at water holes when mothers and young calves felt threatened. *But the young bull elephants of Planesberg were going on a rampage for no reason.*

Officials came up with a possible reason for this aberrant behavior. In the late 1970s, Planesberg became a pioneer in the restocking of animals and baby elephants that would have been marked for slaughtering in other parks (as part of the animal cull to keep animal populations manageable). These animals were instead moved to Planesberg along with only two adult females to care for seventy or more junior elephants.

Clive Walker, chairman of the Rhino and Elephant Foundation of Africa, believes the problem goes back to the childhood trauma suffered by these elephants and to the lack of parental authority throughout their formative years. As babies, these elephants watched their parents being slaughtered and then were trucked off to new, unfamiliar surroundings.

Other South African officials believe the problem has a more biological explanation. The sudden surge of hormones in adolescent elephants produces aggressive behavior that normally would be checked by older males, no longer present in the herd.

During this all-important first year, the foundations for conscience are laid down. And in the first year of life, children learn the forerunners of casaul thinking. That is, they learn to wait, to plan ahead, and importantly, to view others as helpful. During these early months, the brain is being "hardwired" for a lifetime.

All abused animals have much in common when they grow to adulthood. Others are viewed as harmful, there is no conscience, and there is an inability to plan ahead. The neurons, awash in chemicals of rage and rejection, simply do not work right. Most severely disturbed children have thought disorders.

Thus, dangerous individuals threaten the herd, and whoever stands in their way will be gored.

© 1995 Foster W. Cline, M.D.

Foster Cline Answers Your Questions

VOL. 11, No. 1

Question

My six-year-old has made many new friends at school and wants to visit their homes. I find when I let her visit, the parents have such different expectations that they do not meet my standards. Recently she visited a friend who attends our church and both parents seem great, but they left my son and their own alone for twenty minutes or so while running an errand! I would never have guessed this would have happened. Now I am concerned about assessing any parent's judgment. Please give me guidance on this.

Foster's Answer

Hey, frankly, I'm pretty sure you and I are the only ones with really great standards, and sometimes I worry about you!

Seriously, however, we can always be surprised at people's goofiness no matter how well we know them. I surprise myself now and then with my own lapses of judgment! I think the problem is that you want to be sure about something about which you can have no certainty. You want rules to cover all bases so you will not have a risk. But risk is part of life; there is no certainty.

It is better to simply and nonjudgmentally ask how the other parents feel about a subject. We might say something like: "I've always had a problem leaving kids this young unsupervised, and I'm wondering how you feel?"

As long as we say where we stand, and give others space to make their own decisions, we can ask about anything: TV time and content, friends, use of alcohol, driving, etc.

As your child gets older, you can hope that she will be around others who have standards different than your own so she will talk about that with you, and you can share your own thoughts and observations. The beauty of it all is that if you mutually love each other, and if you have a good relationship, she will definitely put your standards inside her and then you will have to worry a lot less about what goes on outside her!

About the time she really knows and locks into your standards, she'll be old enough for adolescence and she can find out how right you are when she plays it differently!

© 1995 Foster W. Cline, M.D.

Commonsense Approaches to ADD
By Jim Fay

VOL. 11, NO. 2

How can I get this kid to be responsible for anything, let alone his schoolwork? He can't remember anything. He's driving me insane! He can't even remember why he's heading for the bathroom.

I bet you recognize the person saying this is to be a parent of a child who's been diagnosed as having Attention Deficit Disorder.

Parents of these children are among the most frustrated parents I have ever known. It doesn't help that much of the common knowledge about children who suffer from Attention Deficit Disorder says they can't remember and can't concentrate for any prolonged period of time.

Fortunately, many of the recent discoveries about Attention Deficit Disorder show that these kids *can* remember. They *can* concentrate. However, they have more difficulty than other children. The good news is that there is hope for these children. They can be motivated to remember, concentrate, and learn from the consequences of their mistakes.

One of the causes for Attention Deficit Disorder is a low level of two brain chemicals, noradrenaline and dopamine. These chemicals assist the firing of the neurons in the brain. Neurons fire slower when these chemicals are at a low level, causing kids to feel "bored."

Children with Attention Deficit Disorder often suffer from hyperactivity because, when they feel bored, they automatically increase their activity levels to a high pitch in order to feel normal. At the same time, memory and attention decrease. These kids seem to be able to spend hours involved in video games when they can't seem to concentrate on learning or responsibilities.

Since drug therapy alone is usually not successful with these children, the solution to this problem often involves a combination of drug therapy and changes in the way parents work with their children. It is helpful to level out the child's reactions and ability to think and remember.

The parenting-style changes include a willingness on the part of the parent to work with determination on only one behavior at a time. This shows children that the parent can and will be successful in expecting responsible behavior.

When this approach is used, a ripple effect takes place. Parents who are willing to focus most of their energy on helping the child change only one behavior at a time find success more quickly with each new behavior they tackle.

There are four steps parents can use to initiate improvement in behavior. Parents who master these four steps will see dramatic changes. Each step will be easier than the last. It is essential that parents move to the next step only after total mastery of the previous step. This is the secret to success in this process.

Step One: Roger does his chores.
Roger learns to complete chores without reminders. He must believe his parents think successful completion of chores is the only important thing in the world.

To accomplish this the parent says, "Your chores are important. I expect you to do them without reminders before your next meal. Your next meal may come today, tomorrow, or Saturday, you decide."

It works best to start this with Roger at a time close to the dinner hour so the consequence for not remembering the chores is available in a timely fashion. Remember, there are to be no reminders and no reasoning or arguing with the child about the fairness of the situation.

Most children will argue, bargain, and manipulate at this point. It is crucial that the parent not give in. Be prepared to say over and over, "I'm sure this doesn't feel fair, and you will eat when the chores are done."

Step Two: Roger learns to go to time-out.

Off to your room, Roger. Please return when you can be sweet. Thank you.

In this second step, the child learns that the parent means business when sending the child to time-out. Once more, work on only this problem until there is success. Some parents have seen success in hiring an older neighborhood child to keep their youngster in his room. It is even better when the child pays for this service with either money or his personal toys.

Step Three: Roger learns to have only "good minutes" in the classroom.
In this step the parent tells Roger that school and learning are privileges. The parent and Roger meet with the teacher and agree that Roger is to learn to sit in class without bothering the other students or interrupting the teacher.

The parent backs the teacher by saying, "If Roger cannot go to time-out in a pleasant way, call this phone number and someone will pick him up and take him home. We will not complain or lecture him. However, he will do some chores to make up for the inconvenience."

Step Four: Roger completes classroom assignments.
This step requires a foolproof communication system between teacher and parent. At this point the parent says to Roger, "Now, are you ready to start doing your school assignments? We expect them to be done at school. Any assignments not completed at school will be supervised at home. Each supervised assignment will require a payment on your part of one chore. This will give me time to supervise the assignment."

Many parents have been successful treating Attention Deficit Disorder with this method. It is most helpful to use the services of a pediatrician for advice regarding drug therapy in making this process more workable.

© 1995 Jim Fay

Let Me Help Your Child Have Some Problems
By Jim Fay

VOL. 11, NO. 3

Have you ever known parents who were very responsible and miserable because their children were very irresponsible and happy? We see this more and more. I often have calls from parents who say their children just want to sleep in each day and hang out with their friends. They don't seem motivated to get a job during the summer months while they are out of school.

These parents want me to tell them what to say to their kids. It is usually stated to me in this manner: "He really has a problem, but no matter how we talk to him or complain or try to tell him how important it is for him to get a job, it never seems to have any effect upon him."

Of course not. He doesn't have a problem. The parents have the problem. The only problem the youngster sees is that of having to listen to complaining parents. That problem can be handled easily. Tune out and turn off and the problem is solved.

The rest of his life is running quite well, thank you. He has a roof over his head, he has food in his stomach. He has time for his friends. He has transportation, free utilities, and no federal income taxes or responsibilities. Why would anyone want to make any changes to this perfect world? Doesn't everyone wish to live the life of the idle rich?

This young man does have a problem that neither he nor his parents have recognized. The problem is having parents who are very responsible to the extent of satisfying all of his needs, including total comfort. If his parents do not change their ways, he will, most likely, become conditioned to believe this is his rightful place in life and that his parents are duty-bound to provide for him.

I have watched these situations. The parents usually become more and more responsible and miserable while the child becomes increasingly irresponsible and unmotivated to change. The parents work harder and harder to try to make these children happy and satisfied.

The children don't feel they have problems. In addition, the kids typically become more resentful of the parents' complaints and more dissatisfied with the level of service and support the parents provide.

These children often become selfish and nasty to their parents, being pleasant or loving only when they want the parents to give them something.

Raising a Spoiled Child

I know a very nice man who can truly say he has given his children everything they have ever asked for. The more rejecting his daughter is, the more he gives her. The more he gives her, the more she demands. He can never do enough to satisfy her. He is now a guilt-ridden, miserable puppet and she is pulling the strings.

The following incident illustrates how spoiled she has become. Her grandmother took her to the airport for a trip and stayed with her until she was on the plane. However, the flight developed problems and was canceled.

The girl called her grandmother to come a long distance back to the airport, take her to her home, put her up for the night, and take her back to the airport. Grandmother actually made three long trips to the airport to help this youngster. The girl never has thanked the grandmother for her sacrifices.

The daughter was furious. She told her dad that Grandma was stupid for leaving the airport in the first place. She demanded to know what they were going to do to make this up to her. Unfortunately, Dad made a huge mistake by answering, "We will think about it." This gave her the upper hand. She then called Dad and demanded to know what Dad and Grandma were going to do for her to make up for treating her so poorly.

Dad should have gone on the offensive immediately by saying, "Sweetie, I'm sorry, but you have this mixed up. Your grandmother is the one who was mistreated. You need to be thanking your grandmother for her sacrifices and asking if she might ever be willing to risk helping you out in the future."

She's Training to Become an "Ex"

I hope this girl enjoys the next few years. It won't be long before she will have to face the real world, where there will be fewer people who are willing to be treated like she treats her parents. There are strong possibilities that she will be an "ex"—frequently known as an ex-wife, ex-employee, ex-friend, etc. The prospect for her having a happy life is not good.

She Needs Some Problems

Her parents can turn this unfortunate situation around, but not without paying a price. The price of success here is going to be a period of nastiness on the part of the girl as she sees her actions becoming problems for herself, not for the people around her.

Her parents must start taking care of themselves and tending to their own needs instead of being so indulgent about hers. The next time she needs transportation, she needs to hear, "Oh, Sweetie, that wasn't in my plans, especially in view of how it worked out for us last time. Try us again sometime."

She probably will go into attack mode with, "How am I supposed to get there then? You know this is important. I promised my friends. You don't want me to let them down, do you?"

The parents are going to have to remain strong. They can answer, "I don't know, Sweetie. I know this is important to you and I hope you can work it out."

As you can expect, she will be angry and throw a huge fit. This is going to be a real test for the parents. If they have the courage to stand their ground, the line is now drawn in the sand. The daughter can expect that things are going to change.

Create a Matching Funds Program

The next step is to stop providing everything this girl asks for. She needs to learn that we get what we want by earning it. A matching funds program is an excellent way to do this.

It won't be long before this youngster comes to her father with, "Dad, the reason I'm not winning the tennis matches is that I have the wrong kind of shoes. Now I know what I need and they only cost $249. We can pick them up on Saturday when we go into town. And, by the way, I need a new tennis racket."

"That sounds great, Sweetie. In the past I have been providing those things, but now I've learned something new. I've learned that kids need to learn how the real world works before they get out into it. So, I'm going to start helping you learn about that by letting you earn what you get so you won't be too surprised when you leave home and are independent.

"However, I still want to help you get what you want, so this time I'll contribute 40 percent toward the new shoes and 20 percent toward the new racket. Come see me when you have the rest of the money, and we can go shopping."

This new program is not going to sit well with the daughter, and we can expect her to throw another fit. This new stand will take courage on Dad's part, because the daughter will try every trick she knows to get her way. But the results will be worth it. She will wear those shoes with a different kind of pride. And she will be better prepared for the real world.

If Dad continues this program, it won't be too long before this youngster comes to him with questions about how he can help her through matching funds, rather than with demands that he give her everything she wants.

Parents who are best at helping their children are parents who know it is a greater gift to prepare their children to support themselves than it is to leave them a good inheritance. You and I both know the girl in this story would make very short work of a good inheritance. She desperately needs to learn how to support herself, especially if she doesn't change her attitudes. I don't see any long-term relationships or marriages in her future.

Your Best Expressions of Love
• Love them enough to set firm yet reasonable limits.
• Love them enough to say no in a nice way.
• Love them enough to refuse their demands.

- Love them enough to let them make mistakes and learn from experience.
- Love them enough to expect them to do chores as a contribution to the family.
- Love them enough to make them earn the special things they want.
- Love them enough to expect them to treat you as well as you treat them.

The Love and Logic Institute is dedicated to supporting you as you express your love in these ways.

© 1995 Jim Fay

CLINE'S CORNER

The ADD Epidemic: An Overview
By Foster W. Cline, M.D.

VOL. 11, NO. 3

Because there is an epidemic of ADD—Attention Deficit Disorder—in the United States, Jim and I are often asked about the accuracy or specificity of this diagnosis. I thought it would be a good idea to look at this ubiquitous diagnosis.

ADD is a very specific disorder of attention. It is diagnosed as such in the *Diagnostic and Statistical Manual of the American Psychiatric Association* as follows:

- Inattentive type: Not giving close attention; not listening; not giving attention to details; not following through on instructions; difficulty organizing tasks; easily distracted; and often forgetful.
- Hyperactive/impulsive type: Fidgets, runs about or climbs excessively; has problems playing quietly; acts as if driven by a motor; has difficulty awaiting his turn; and butts into conversations.
- The symptoms were present before age seven and they are present in two or more settings. There must be clear evidence

of clinically significant impairment in social, academic, or occupational functioning.

Note that we are not talking about a disobedient child. We are talking about a child who can be and often is frustrating to a parent. We are talking about a child who has difficulty in focus, follow-through, attention, and sometimes movement.

The impulsive problems of ADD cause a diagnostic problem, for many behavior-disordered, out-of-control, and obnoxious children have impulse problems. They simply don't mind and don't listen to their parents. Unfortunately, many of these children are labeled ADD. And, of course, it is easier for some parents to be convinced they have an ADD kid than a kid who is simply beyond their control, often because of parenting techniques.

There is another diagnostic problem. In today's world, many children with one type or another of learning disorder are now, according to some authorities, ADD. Thus, various types of learning disorders and ADD tend to be rolled up into the same ball of wax. This can be very confusing.

So What's ADD and What's Not?

Because the lines blur, I have the following eight guidelines I use. Naturally, all of the guidelines may not be present, but the more that are, the more likely it is that the problem is ADD:

1. A boy (three males have ADD for every female).
2. Always present before age seven.
3. Messy handwriting compared with other children the same age.
4. Parents have good parenting techniques and the child's siblings are normal.
5. The child is fun to be around one-to-one. In other words, when someone is there to provide focus, the child is genuinely likable.
6. The biggest problems occur in social situations where lack of structure allows the child to fragment: on the school bus, on the playground, etc.

7. The child has a definite good response to Ritalin or other stimulants that help focus attention.
8. The child has the problem both at home and at school.

There are many children who do not have true ADD because:

- They give their parents a hard time but do well in school or with other caretaking adults (likely parenting problem).
- They do well with parents but poorly in school (look for learning or social problems).
- They have no problem with focus, do well in school, but have problems with other children or authority figures (look for oppositional disorder or conduct disorders).

Overall, the more normal the siblings are, the more likely the problem is within the child him- or herself. If the parents have trouble with all their children, the more likely it is a parenting problem.

What Causes ADD?

True isolated ADD is a brain problem—a hardwiring problem. Generally, ADD is considered to be a genetic problem, and often one parent had ADD symptoms as a child. Therefore, ADD is present very early in life.

ADD may be a symptom complex with a variety of other primary problems. For instance, children get overly active when they get anxious. Chronic anxiety, often perhaps from lack of parental structure, causes impulse-ridden, acting-out children who are often out of control and who often have trouble with authority figures.

Attention Deficit Disorder is part of the symptom complex of many organic developmental disorders, and may be part of Reactive Attachment Disorder.

© 1995 Foster W. Cline, M.D.

FOSTER CLINE ANSWERS YOUR QUESTIONS

Santa Claus: To Tell or Not to Tell?

VOL. 11, NO. 3

Question

Dr. Cline, what did you tell your own children about Santa Claus? Did they believe in Santa and, if so, how and when did you "break the news"? If they always knew "reality," then how did you create this awareness with them at an early age?

Dr. Cline's Answer

In our home, we have enjoyed three generations of the Santa Claus myth. I well remember seeing Santa as a youth at the Masons' Christmas party. I was surprised as a little guy that when I sat on Santa's lap, his hands looked like Dad's hands, and he even had the same ring! Imagine that! Yet he lived at the North Pole.

It took a few years of puzzling about that one before, with some pride in my dad, I admitted the old guy had really fooled me. And I was sitting right on his lap, for heaven's sake! I don't know now, as an adult, whether his makeup was all that good or I was just a dumb kid. Probably the latter!

When Robin was a little girl, we had a little routine every Christmas Eve. I took a flashlight out on the front lawn, over on the other side of a little pond, and covered it with red cellophane. Then I would run and jump along through the snow, swinging the light in great overhead arcs. This was supposed to be a bounding Rudolph.

Actually, for four years it worked out great. Then came the year, when she was about five, that she said, "I can hardly wait for Dad ... I mean Rudolph ... to come past tonight." My daughter was a lot smarter of a kid than I ever was!

Now I play the same game with my granddaughters. The oldest one, when she was three, took one look at Rudolph and surprised us all by panicking and running, screaming, up to her bed. "I've got to be asleep! I've got to be asleep!"

She didn't want to take any chances on missing out on the presents because she wasn't asleep in her bed, just like the poem says she should be. Last winter, at age five, she was very excited we would be playing the same old routine with her little sister, and told me to be sure to wear boots.

I have little patience with folks who worry about the harm being done to children by passing along the Santa myth. If they think their child will be ruined by believing in this for a few years and then finding out it was just a wonderful make-believe, then they probably have a pretty fragile child.

As far as I am concerned, the Santa myth is preparation for life. All of us believe in myths (often as adults) and then find out we were mistaken or working with inadequate data. (I grew up thinking politicians wanted to help America and presidents were honest.) And then, like children, we need to admit we have reached a new conclusion based on new data.

We never "broke the news" to our children, but let them discover it on their own and teach us. And we were always properly doubtful about their new conclusions—just like it always works in life when one attempts to convey new information to those who hold the old beliefs.

Of course, we never forgot the real reason for celebrating Christmas, but that is a completely different issue. I doubt Christ would have trouble making room for Santa.

Labels Don't Make Kids Behave Better
By Jim Fay
Vol. 11, No. 4

I frequently have parents come to me and say, "My son was just diagnosed with ADHD." I sense a feeling of relief on their part. I often feel an odd sort of glow surrounding these parents.

It's almost as if they are saying, "Now he will be okay because we know what's wrong with him. He's been labeled with Attention Deficit Hyperactive Disorder."

The bad news is that there are thousands of kids carrying around labels such as Learning Disabled, Attention Deficit Disordered, Oppositional Defiant, Conduct Disordered, etc. And these kids are not one bit better off today than they were the day they were diagnosed and labeled.

Unfortunately, many of these kids are actually worse off today, because their label became a built-in excuse. These kids go through life thinking, "How can I learn? I'm disabled." "How can anyone expect me to be responsible? I'm ADHD."

All this kind of thinking accomplishes is to help people intensify their feelings of helplessness. Eventually it produces a "victim mentality."

An additional problem created by "label thinking" is that it severely reduces the effectiveness of the adults who work with the problem child. It is easy for the adults to fall into the trap of trying to solve the label instead of solving specific problem behaviors. Consider the following example.

Mrs. Jones comes to me and says, "What do I do with Roger? He has ADHD." It is tempting to talk about ADHD and all its problems, but what good is that going to do for Roger or his mom?

If I am going to provide some real help, I should ask, "What is the specific problem you want to solve?"

"Well, he's not so bad when he takes his medication, but what do I do with him when he is not on the medication?"

This question is still too general. I will not be able to help until I can get Mom to focus upon one specific behavior, so I try, "What time of day does this problem present itself?"

Mom comes back with, "It's the morning. It's the time when I am trying to get him out of bed, dressed, fed, and out of the house on his way to school. That's when he just about drives me crazy!"

Now we are getting closer to finding some help for her, but practical help will not come until I can get her to break down that time of day into specific behaviors. I try, "What are the specific things you need him to do? Let's make a list of them. After we make the list, we will prioritize the list and then I'll give you some specific advice."

"That's easy," says Mom. "First, I have to get him out of bed, then get him to dress, then get him to come to breakfast, eat his breakfast, find all of his school supplies, and then get him out the door on time."

Ah! Now we are headed for solutions! Mom can be successful if she can take control of each of these problems instead of thinking of one big problem—that this child has Attention Deficit Hyperactive Disorder.

Let's take these problems one at a time, remembering that solutions for these individual problems are the same for all kids regardless of their labels or disabilities.

Getting Him Out of Bed

Buy him an alarm clock. Teach him how to set it. Let him decide how much time he needs to get ready for school, and let him set the alarm. Assure him you will never wake him up again, that it is up to him.

Call the school and let them know you are having a Love and Logic training session. Ask the teacher to give him trouble if he is late or if he misses school the next day. Tell the teacher you won't be writing him an excuse for being either late or absent. Now go to sleep after praying for him to sleep through the alarm.

Here are some options if he sleeps through his alarm:

1. He pays for a cab to take himself to school.
2. He gets to school under his own power.
3. He stays in his room all day and pays for a baby-sitter to take care of him. (You were going shopping or to work and can't do this for him.) You have not lived until your child sleeps through the alarm and wakes up and finds Mabel, the baby-sitter from hell, sitting at the kitchen table saying, "I'm your baby-sitter today. Your mother says you will be paying for my services."

How does a child pay if he doesn't have money? He pays with toys or personal possessions.

Getting Him to Dress

Call the school once more and let them know he will be choosing his own clothes and his parents are not responsible for his looks. Actually, that is not necessary. Teachers see all kinds of costumes these days and don't spend much time judging parents based upon the dress of kids.

Give the youngster a couple of choices of outfits and let him decide. Remind him he doesn't need to be totally dressed when he leaves the house, that you will have a grocery bag available in case he has to take some of his clothes along.

Eating Breakfast

Call the school in advance and let them know you are having a Love and Logic training session and there is a possibility the child will appear at school claiming he was sent without his breakfast. Tell the teacher his breakfast will be available and his eating it will depend on him getting ready to go on time.

Remind the teacher that children don't die if they miss their morning meal. They get hungry, which is the very consequence that teaches them to eat. The teacher can be a big help if he/she will just say, "Yes, it is so sad to miss breakfast, but I am sure lunch will make life better."

Remembering Lunch, Homework, etc.

It is important that parents provide no reminders. Tell your child you won't be reminding and nagging him to do a good job of getting ready for school and that in return he won't have to remind you to go to work, do a good job, or pay the rent.

Being prepared to leave for school with all the "school stuff" must be the total responsibility of the child. Children do not take responsibility for things their parents worry about. They think to themselves, "My mom has that concern well in hand. No sense in both of us worrying about it."

In the likely event this child does forget something, allow him to experience the consequences. Don't rescue, but don't give lectures or be mean about it. Simply express your sincere sadness and wish him luck in the future.

You will probably experience some first-class begging or manipulating at this point. He will tell you all the horrible things that will happen to him if you don't bring his assignment or permission slip to school. You will probably be drawn into feeling as though you are a terrible person who doesn't care.

Go "Brain Dead" When Kids Manipulate

Don't reason or argue with a begging or manipulating child. Don't explain why it is good for him to learn from experience. Use the Love and Logic technique of going brain dead, saying the same thing over and over so you don't give the youngster the upper hand. Example:

SON: "But, Mom, I'm going to get a bad grade if you don't bring my homework."

MOM: "I bet it looks that way."

SON: "But the teacher is really going to be mad."

MOM: "I bet it looks that way."

SON: "You want me to get good grades and you don't help?"

MOM: "I bet it looks that way.

SON: "If you loved me, you'd bring it."

MOM: "Nice try, Son. I'll see you at home. I hope things work out for you."

Mom can now think to herself, "Good, he's just had one more great practice session with consequences, and as a result he's one step closer to success."

Notice that in this example the parent had a very chaotic situation with a child who was out of control. An expert evaluated the child and labeled him as having an Attention Deficit Hyperactive Disorder. Medication was prescribed.

Yet the problem still existed until the parent broke it down into manageable parts and then created a plan for solving each individual part.

Love and Logic parents and teachers focus their efforts upon specific behaviors, not labels. Labels alone have never provided solutions.

© 1996 Jim Fay

CLINE'S CORNER

Rules for Rescue
By Foster W. Cline, M.D.

VOL. 11, NO. 4

Love and Logic teaches that children learn through consequences. Love and Logic parents know rescue makes children weaker, and consequences allow children to learn from their mistakes and grow to be thoughtful adults.

Love and Logic parents allow mistakes and failures, knowing these are excellent learning opportunities and that, basically, children (and populations of people) who are protected from consequences grow to be irresponsible and blaming of others. And yet ...

There are those times when our kids are in a jam of one kind or another and every fiber of our beings says, *For heaven's sake, lend a hand to help him or her out of this.*

There are times that it is safe, effective, and wise—more than that, it is just ... nice—to help our kids out of jams they get into. Sometimes I've found Love and Logic parents want so much not to be Helicopter parents that they stand by when they could be lending a helping hand that would make them and their child both feel a lot better—about each other and about life.

Our federal government is in the same bind. It is dealing, on a federal level, with Helicopter or Hovering parent issues. How much assistance, Medicare, Medicaid, SSI, food stamps, is enough, and how much is too much? How much helps people, and how much keeps them dependent on government handouts?

Luckily, the rules for rescue apply across the board. They apply to our homes, to our businesses, to our neighbors, and to the government. So let's look at the situations where rescue is okay, and the situations where it is not.

Here is an actual situation we will look at. As I discuss the rescue rules, you come to a conclusion whether I should rescue the kid.

It was a snowy evening. My sixteen-year-old son wanted to go out with a friend, taking his friend's car, with his friend driving on our mountain roads, and go down to Denver. I told Andy I didn't think it was a good idea. It was cold and snowing, and the roads were icy, and I'd bag the evening if I were him. He decided to go out anyway. At about midnight, I got a call.

"Dad, Bill and I are in the ditch over by the Henderson house. Will you please come winch us out?"

I rub the sleep out of my eyes. I think about the warm bed and wife I'd have to leave. I say, "Andy, I thought Kirk was driving. In the first place, whether I come or not, aren't you phoning the wrong dad?"

"Yeah, I know, Dad, but if his dad came down he'd get mad at Kirk and jaw at him about it for days, and I'd really appreciate your doing it."

Should I go winch him out? Let's look at the rescue rules. First, there are two basic types of rescue. In metaphor we will call them:

• Guardian Angel rescue rules
• Milk of Human Kindness rescue rules

Like it or not, as parents we sometimes must function as our kids' Guardian Angels. I have discussed Guardian Angel rules before, so I am going to be brief here. Guardian Angels:

• Come into play when life and limb are in definite danger. They don't mess with the small stuff.

- Are invisible.
- Are fairly unreliable and no one takes them for granted. (I'll be driving real reckless tonight because I have George in the passenger seat.)
- Allow death to occur if someone knowingly plays the odds. (If one loads a six-shooter with three bullets, spins the chamber, puts the barrel to one's head, and pulls the trigger, one has a 50 percent chance of death, Guardian Angel or no Guardian Angel!)

If life and limb are in danger from a stupid mistake, it is always good to try to save the child's life. Parents should do something unobtrusively, behind the scenes, or in such a way that the child will know he or she cannot depend on rescue. Luckily, life-and-limb issues don't come up very often for most of us.

Is Andy's problem a Guardian Angel rescue problem? *No!* His life and limb are not in danger. He made it to a phone. He wouldn't freeze in the car overnight. He'd live no matter what I do.

So ... now we come to the Milk of Human Kindness rescue rules:

- When a person is in a jam through no fault of his or her own, it helps our own souls grow to go out of our way to help out. This is true for both chronic and acute problems.
- When people cause themselves a problem, or are at least partially responsible for the mess they are in, never go more than halfway. This is a very important rule and bears on many federal government issues of rescue. (Example: A child—or group of people—chronically needs help because of bad decisions. They must help themselves out of the mess, at least 51 percent of the way, before they have one finger lifted for them!)
- If the problem that people cause themselves is acute or new, it is generally safe to go all-out to save them.
- Regardless of whether the problem is acute or chronic, self-inflicted or not, no one should be helped if he or she demands or expects help. To help such people only leads to more chronic

problems for them, while the helpers, not given the choice to give, become resentful.

So, should I help Andy out of the snowdrift at midnight? It is not a Guardian Angel problem. This is an acute problem. He does not have a history of calling for help and making poor decisions that would turn this individual issue into a chronic problem. He did not demand help. He asked nicely and hopefully.

Will I get out of bed to help this kid? You bet. And then comes the hard part—not saying I told you so. Sure enough, when I said, "Well, this is a bad curve, it would be easy to slip into the ditch on this one ... ," he said, "Yeah, but we shouldn't have been out in this storm tonight anyway." And I said to myself, "Good thinking, kid!"

VOLUME
12

How to Raise a Toddler Tyrant

By Jim Fay

VOL. 12, NO. 1

Three-year-old Stephanie is not so cute anymore. She refuses to cooperate with her parents and is constantly throwing fits when she doesn't get her way.

Today is no different. Her father asked her if she would like to get in the car so the family could go home. Stephanie refused. Her parents spent the next fifteen minutes begging and pleading with her to do it on her own. She finally agreed, but they would have to buy her a soda on the way home.

It took these loving parents less than three years to create a tyrant. How did they do it? Judging from this example it appears the parents are trying to be more open and democratic than their own parents. However, it seems they have gone to the opposite extreme, allowing Stephanie to run their home.

You can probably predict what Stephanie is going to be like as a teenager. Her demands will be greater. Instead of being bought off by a soda, it will probably be a new car she demands upon turning sixteen. When she gets into trouble the parents may want to blame educators, television, or the declining morality of society instead of looking at their failure to set firm limits for Stephanie when she was young.

I watched another parent in the airport systematically producing a youngster who would become a major frustration later in life. During a one-hour period, this mother issued at least eighty different demands to a three-year-old boy. They went on and on:

"Come back here, Mark!"
"Don't go over there, Mark!"
"Why don't you ever listen, Mark?"
"I mean it, Mark!"
"Don't run, Mark!"
"You're going to get hurt, Mark!"

Mark eventually found his way to where I was seated. He was smiling at me while ignoring his mother, which is exactly what he had been doing for the last forty-five minutes. During this time, Mom had issued order after order. Unfortunately, she never enforced one of them.

Just then I heard her yell, "Mark, you get away from that man! You get over here this instant!"

I smiled down at Mark and said, "Hey, Mark. What is your mom going to do if you don't get over there?" He looked up at me and grinned. "She not goin' to do nothin'." And then his eye twinkled and his grin became wider. He and I had a special understanding about who ran his home, and it wasn't his mother.

It turned out he was right. She finally came over to me, apologizing. "I'm sorry he's bothering you, but you know how three-year-olds are. They just won't listen to one thing you tell them."

I could just imagine how she will talk to her friends when Mark is fifteen. She will be telling them how difficult and frustrating he is, but by then she will have a new excuse. She will probably blame his bad behavior on the fact that he is a teenager. Maybe she will even tell her friends, "You know how teens are. They won't listen to a think you say."

These situations are tragedies. They don't need to happen. We can raise kids who are well-behaved and who listen to and respect their parents.

If children were meant to run the home they would be born larger. You can avoid raising a tyrant if you are willing to:

1. Say it once. Never warn or remind.

Parents who raise tyrants like Stephanie usually teach their kids that they don't have to listen the first time. They do this by failing to provide a consequence when the child does not respond. Instead they keep reminding and eventually either get mad or give up.

Tell your toddler what you expect. Do not say it again. If he/she fails to comply, sing the child to their room with, "Uh, oh. Bad decision. This is so sad. A little bedroom time's coming up here." If you've timed the trip to the bedroom right, the child should be going into the room about the same time you finish your little song.

Yes, this means the child is to be picked up and taken into the room without warning and without anger. Your singing helps the child see it is not a problem for the adult, but one for them. And yes, it's legal. And no, it won't hurt the child in any way. What hurts the child is to learn that the parent makes idle threats.

Time-out in the room starts only after the child is calm. Thinking does not go on while the temper tantrum is going on, so give the child ten minutes to do some heavy duty thinking about his/her bad decision. Lay on lots of love when the child returns. Be sad that they made a bad decision, and reassure the child of your love.

This process needs to be repeated over and over. Be consistent, and you will be rewarded.

2. Remember the golden rule of Love and Logic.

Love and Logic parents have a golden rule for their children: "You get to be around me when you behave and are fun to be around. You get to be by yourself when you're not."

One Love and Logic parent put a full-length mirror in her child's room. When the child acted up, she would calmly say, "Honey, there is someone in your mirror who would appreciate that a lot more than me. I'll see you when you are sweeter."

© 1996 Jim Fay

Anger: When It's Appropriate
By Foster W. Cline, M.D., and Jim Fay

As a general rule, the decision about whether to use anger in our dealings with our children hinges on the issue of separation of problems. Kids' problems should always be met with our empathy. They got themselves into the mess. The gain in their responsibility can be won only if we commiserate with them, not if we shout at them when they're working it out.

If our kids' mistakes only hurt them and not us—if they trip and fall, or throw their fists and come home with a black eye, or fail half a dozen classes at school—then our anger makes the problem worse.

It's a lot like the hot-rodding husband who hugs bumpers in the fast lane and pushes the needle into the red zone. If his wife screams, "Honey, stop it! You're doing seventy-five!" it only makes him angry. Because he's the one driving, he thinks the speed is his concern, and he resents interference from his wife.

But if the wife says, "Honey, I don't want to die," she's bringing her own welfare into the equation. Her anger is understandable and effective. He can take *that*.

When our kids do something that affects us directly—lose our tools, leave their trikes in the driveway, fail to put our things away after using them—then it's okay for us to get a bit huffy. They will recognize that we're angry because their misbehavior has affected us.

Little Barb, in her eagerness to cut out paper dolls, broke her mom's scissors. Mom, realizing that anger was entirely appropriate, said, "Barb, I'm so angry I can't see straight. Now I can't even use my own scissors. I expect you to do something to make this right. Be prepared to tell me before you go to bed tonight what you're going to do." Notice that Mom did not demean the child with her anger; she didn't tell Barb how stupid and irresponsible she was. Instead, she focused on how Barb's action affected her and the need for a solution.

Anger is also generally appropriate if we've made a rational decision to use it. Occasionally, kids need to be read a sixty-second riot act. They need a show of anger. We can ponder these options: "Do I want to isolate my child? Or do I want to talk it over with him or her to do some problem-solving? Or do I think this child needs a sixty-second rant and a hug afterward, with me saying, 'The reason I'm so angry, Dear, is because you're the type of kid who could handle the situation so much better.'"

The decision to use anger must be dispassionate, not a flying-off-the-handle, finger-poking-in-the-chest brawl-out. Generally speaking, anger should be used only when our children's behavior directly affects us.

One note of caution: We should not use anger so often that it becomes an expected emotion. Once kids get used to a particular emotion—be it shame, anger, guilt, or love—that expected emotion becomes the emotion of choice.

From Parenting with Love and Logic:
Teaching Children Responsibility.
© *1990 Foster W. Cline, M.D., and Jim Fay*

CLINE'S CORNER

The Importance of Firm Limits and Consistency
By Foster W. Cline, M.D.
VOL. 12, NO. 1

The place was awesomely beautiful, billing itself the Garden City. I thought this was a little pretentious until I got there. Then I discovered the truth of the statement. It is a city of several million, and is truly spotless. No trash on the streets, no graffiti, no litter.

It has modern shopping centers, long green beltways, and large, trash-free parks. In the center of the downtown area there is a beautiful mosaic tile mural that stretches for a block. It glistens unvandalized for everyone to enjoy.

For an American, it was a pretty sobering experience, for it wasn't an American city. It was a city like we all wish in our hearts that our cities could be.

Unlike America, where our largest social expenditure goes toward fighting the drug problem, the city is virtually drug-free. Money is spent on parks, and what may be the world's premier zoo, where visitors are encouraged to walk among the animals. I was able to touch kangaroos and monkeys and actually become a part of the animal landscape.

You may be wondering if such a place actually exists. I wouldn't have believed it myself, but it does. It's Singapore. How can a large metropolitan city be drug- and litter-free?

How can there be a zoo where people are able to walk with the animals—without the animals being seriously harmed by being around bratty kids and adults who feed the animals pennies? How can there be a city of parks and greenbelts without litter?

I found the answer is actually pretty simple. Unlike America, in Singapore it really is a crime to break the law! Putting it simply, Singapore's laws are for real, and people are held totally accountable for their actions.

At the same time, seemingly paradoxically, businessmen love Singapore because of its relative business freedom. Economic growth has therefore taken place at an astonishing rate.

The loving and effective raising of children is so much like wise governing. For wise parents, no means no and yes means yes. That's the way it is in Singapore. More freedom, but firmer limits, and absolute consistency of consequences.

Singapore, as far as I know, is the only country in the world that has the following written in red on its customs declarations: *In Singapore, trafficking in drugs brings death.* Somehow as I sat on the plane at 30,000 feet, I had the feeling those boys played for keeps—that it wasn't a threat, as it is in the United States, but a statement.

When I arrived in Singapore, and the luggage was all checked with an electronic sniffer for an airborne molecule of drugs, I was even more certain.

No wonder there are beautiful murals and no graffiti downtown. You want to vandalize Singapore? You can, kids, but it will inevitably cost you a public caning. Even the president of the United States found out, much to his surprise, that they really do mean it.

The kids attending the Singapore American School are told this at their first assembly: "Hey, guys, you want to trash cars, do graffiti, mess with the animals in the park? Well, wait until you get back to the States. It's okay to break the law there, but in Singapore, it's a crime to break the law."

A Singaporean woman summed up the situation for me: "Singapore is the best place in the world to live, unless you are a crook. Then it's not fun at all. When I first came here, I was against the caning and the government crackdown. But now I realize they don't have to crack down much because they always are willing to crack down. The only people surprised by this are the Americans. We have relatively little crime. I've completely changed my mind."

I am not suggesting parents start using corporal punishment with their kids. But I am wondering if there is not a philosophical truth that can be learned from Singapore: fewer laws, more freedom, firmer meaningful consistent limits with consequences. That's the way wise parents play it, too.

© *1996 Foster W. Cline, M.D.*

Home Zone or Combat Zone?

By Jim Fay

VOL. 12, No. 2

I don't know why my kid has to argue all the time! We can never have an enjoyable meal in our house now that the kids are teenagers. It doesn't matter what I say, I get nothing but nasty remarks and demands that I get out of their lives. What am I going to do?

I have heard this many times over the past few years. The parents are frustrated and no longer experiencing the joys of parenthood. I usually try to be empathetic, asking what all the arguing is about. I often get a response from the parent such as, "I tell them and tell them not to argue with me, but they won't listen!"

The words "I tell them and tell them" usually give me a preview of the conversation to follow. It becomes obvious to me that the parent has become somewhat terrified of the possible mistakes this youngster could make now that he/she is growing into a teen. In an attempt to forestall impending disaster, the parent has created their own version of the disaster by making lots of threats, many of which cannot be carried out.

These threats are received by the youngster as a direct attack on his/her personal control and independence. Following is a typical example:

DAD: "I don't want you hanging out with Rob and Jeff. If you can't find better friends, you're going to have to start coming straight home after school."

SON: "Hey, my friends are just fine! They're a whole lot better than your sleazy friends who tell kids not to do drugs while they sip on their precious cocktails."

DAD: "Don't you talk to me like that! As long as you live in this house you are going to show a little respect."

SON: "Oh, sure, respect like you show me, always on my case about my friends and how I dress. You talk about respect but don't know how to give any. You're not picking my friends for me."

DAD: "Where is your judgment? Those friends of yours are born losers and you are going to find yourself in a lot of trouble if you keep hanging out with them."

SON: "I can take care of myself. I don't need you messing in my life. I don't have to listen to this. I'm out of here!"

DAD: "That does it. We're going to have some rules around here!"

Conversations That Begin with Threats and End in Disaster
In this situation, Dad tried to help his son avoid a future problem. Dad meant well, but starting any conversation with a threat is a surefire recipe for disaster.

In many families there is a pattern in which parents are afraid the child will make mistakes, so the parents make threats attempting to control the situation. The youngster, feeling a loss of control, fights back.

In some families this cycle repeats itself many times during the day. The intensity of the fights increases. Parents feel less and less control. The child feels less and less love. Both parent and child come to realize their once loving relationship is gone.

Concern Is More Powerful Than Power

Compare the strategy of the father below to the one in the first conversation. This dad is also trying to get his son to think about his choice of friends. He uses sincere questions and a show of concern:

DAD: "Do you ever worry that you might find yourself in the wrong place at the wrong time with Rob and Jeff?"

SON: "What do you mean?"

DAD: "Well, I've been concerned that they have a history of finding themselves in trouble."

SON: "You know I don't do things like that."

DAD: "I know you don't, but I was wondering if you think it would help for you to have a lawyer on retainer just in case you find yourself in a bad spot with them and need someone to bail you out."

SON: "Dad, that's silly. I'm going to be okay."

DAD: "That's probably true; I was just wondering. But would you mind giving it some thought, just for me? Thanks."

Both of these dads wanted their sons to think carefully about their choices of friends. The first dad lost completely, as the teen refused to listen to or think about Dad's concerns. The dad in the second situation has not only gotten his son to think, but also preserved their relationship, as well.

Three Rules Can Run a Home

Parents can have more success with their kids, and avoid creating a combat zone in the home, by limiting the number of rules and eliminating threats. It is far more effective to tell kids your expectations without telling what you are going to do if they are not met. If expectations are not met, it is then most effective to delay the consequence.

One Love and Logic mother left this note on the front door for her eighteen-year-old to see as he left the house one morning:

The door was left unlocked when you came in last night. Please have dinner ready for the family at 6 p.m. Logical consequences are now under consideration regarding the unlocked door. Love, Mom.

I suggest that three rules are usually enough for any home:

RULE 1: Treat your parents with the same respect they treat you.
RULE 2: Do your share of the housework.
RULE 3: Don't make a problem for others in the family.

Consequences for breaking these rules can be designed as necessary.

A Love and Logic mother gives the following example of how this worked for her. Mom was visiting with some of her friends. Thirteen-year-old Marcia got tired of waiting and asked if she could go to the car. Mom agreed, and Marcia hopped off to the car, finding it locked.

She was furious. She screamed at her mother, "Mom, you get your butt out here!" Needless to say, Mom was embarrassed.

Mom applied Rule 3—Don't make a problem for others in the family. In a quiet voice she said, "Marcia, that was such a bad decision. You just made a big problem for me. I'm going to have to think about a consequence. I'll let you know later what it is. In the meantime, try not to worry about it."

Marcia was rather quiet on the way home. As they passed a fast food restaurant she asked if they could stop for a soda. Mom answered that she wouldn't feel very good about buying her a soda after what had just happened.

At home, Marcia actually offered to help with the meal. This gave her a good chance to ask, "Mom, what are you going to do about what I did today?"

"I don't know, Honey. It was pretty upsetting. I'll try to let you know by morning so you don't have to worry too long."

The next morning Mom was able to let Marcia know that doing the laundry on Saturday morning would make up for the problem she had created with her nastiness. She even gave Marcia a choice of doing it on her own or paying someone to supervise her.

There are distinct advantages to stating rules or expectations without telling kids what the consequences for breaking them will be. It gives parents time to think through the problem. It gives parents time to get out of the emotional state. And it keeps parents from becoming locked into a consequence that either can't be enforced or doesn't fit.

There is another advantage: Kids can't argue and create a combat zone when they can't figure out what to argue about.

© *1996 Jim Fay*

CLINE'S CORNER

The World's Most Effective Emotion for Modifying Children's Behavior
By Foster W. Cline, M.D.

VOL. 12, NO. 2

Human beings virtually live for emotion. Christians believe God wants His people to love Him, so emotions are evidently important even to God.

The most requested speakers, the most sought-after entertainers, the world's most highly paid people are those who stimulate our emotions. Emotion keeps the spinal cord from shriveling!

There are a number of emotions that are effective in modifying behavior. Stark terror, for instance, brings quick responses.

But there is another common emotion that is almost as effective as stark terror. This emotion, generally given by adults to kids, motivates children's behavior far more frequently than any other emotion.

Think for a moment. Don't just read on. What's your guess?

You could guess love. However, love is actually slow to motivate behavior. Very loving parents have great kids—or kids you wouldn't take off the shelf. Love even appears not to be that interesting for most of us. When *Jurassic Park* (about dinosaurs dining on humans) and a sweet movie like *Sleepless in Seattle* (about the growth of love) have nearly simultaneous releases, which will be the runaway hit? Give us a dinosaur-eating lawyer in an outhouse any day!

No, the emotion I am writing about is frustration. From a kid's point of view, frustration is an irresistible mix of wonderful emotions: anger and loss of control. No kid could ask for anything better.

As a matter of fact, we all love frustration. Most sitcoms and many comic strips are based on frustrated authority figures—*Sgt. Bilko, Stalag 17, M*A*S*H*, Beetle Bailey*—the list goes on and on.

A beloved children's game based on mock frustration is peek-a-boo: "Oh, no! You see me!" Kids love mock frustration: "Oh, darn, you beat me to the car!"

It is the frustration-relief-frustration behaviors—gambling, golf, etc.—that are actually the most addicting.

Whenever adults show real frustration, they do two wonderful things from the kid's point of view. They give off vibrations of strong emotion, usually anger, and then delightfully declare they have no control over the situation.

Frustration is always loss of control. Obviously, if the adult doesn't have it, the kid does! And this is the irresistible combination for the child. The parent turns red, lights up, gets noisy, and hands control to the child. Now what kid wouldn't want that?

Love and Logic is a method of raising children that best ensures parents are unlikely to feel frustrated. That is one of Love and Logic's great drawing cards. Love and Logic parents may feel sad for their child. They may be empathetic about the consequences the child suffers. But Love and Logic parents are generally too effective to be frustrated.

In a future article I'll discuss why parents are most frequently frustrated, and how Love and Logic parenting ensures the replacement of frustration with other, more useful emotions.

"If I Could Do It All Over Again"
By Jim Fay
VOL. 12, No. 3

Parents often hit me with, "Jim, I know you had fun raising your kids, we hear it in your stories. But what would you do differently if you could try it all over again?"

That's an easy question to answer, because I have learned so much since the kids left home. I also don't have trouble answering that because I've thought about it so many times.

Expressions of Love

First of all, I would have given them a lot more hugs and reminded them more frequently how proud I was to be their father. I too often assumed they knew how much I loved them and besides, I grew up with a father who did not feel right about touching us and bragging to us about what great kids we were. We all found out later that he bragged to everyone else about us. You can't do too much touching, hugging, and expressing your genuine love.

Criticism

I would have spent less time telling them what was wrong with their lives and a lot more time reminding them of their accomplishments. My years of experience have caused me to meet thousands of people who are stymied by their negative beliefs about themselves. Most of these people have taken over their parents' criticism by constantly telling themselves how incapable they are.

The most important concern about criticism is that children who grow up with criticism grow up to be critical adults who are chronically unhappy. They usually only feel good about themselves when they know what is wrong with others.

Have you ever heard of constructive criticism? *There is no such thing!* Kids don't learn from being told what they are doing wrong. They learn when loving adults allow them to learn from experience.

I would have spent more time telling my kids why *I* did things, not why *they* should. I would have spent more time allowing them to make mistakes and then being genuinely sad for them as they lived with the consequences and learned from their mistakes. A little of this does more teaching than a ton of criticism.

Warnings and Threats

"As long as you live in this house you are not going to drink. If I catch you drinking, you're in big trouble!" This kind of warning does no good. Kids who hear this become more stubborn, defiant, or anxious. Instead, parents who state their expectations for their kids in a calm way get better results.

For example, "Josie, you are welcome to drive the family car as long as I don't have to worry about alcohol." Notice that this is not a warning. It is just an enforceable statement.

In the event that Josie uses alcohol, the parent can calmly state, "Josie, I smelled alcohol on your breath last night. What's your guess about the family car?"

"I don't get to use it?"

"Right, Josie. Good thinking."

"Well, when do I get to use it again?"

"I don't know, Josie. I guess that will depend upon when I stop worrying about the use of alcohol. Try not to worry about it."

Needless to say, Josie will do some major worrying at this point. The consequence for her misbehavior came "like a lightning bolt out of the sky."

I met a responsible young man who looked back on his father's parenting style with great admiration, saying, "When I was a teen, I thought my father never gave me any slack. He always punished me when I did something wrong.

"Later, I found out it was not my dad, but me, who put the clamps on my behavior. My dad never warned me about consequences. He just laid them on when I did something wrong. After a while a voice played in my head telling me that if I did something wrong, my dad would do something. I never knew what it was going to be, and I didn't especially want to find out, so I behaved myself instead."

Reduce the Number of Rules

If I were raising kids today, I would replace a lot of our rules with enforceable limits:

"My car will be leaving at 7:30. I can't wait to see if you go with your clothes on your body or in a bag."
"Dinner will be served for the next thirty minutes. Get all you need to make it to the next meal."
"I'll be glad to listen to you when your voice sounds like mine."
"Everyone whose room is clean will be going to the game with us on Saturday."
"I give out allowance every Saturday at 9 a.m. I hope you can make it last for a week."

My house rules would be:

1. *Treat your parents with the same respect with which they treat you.* Mistreatment of the parents will be known as an "energy drain." The child can restore this energy loss by doing some of the parents' regular chores for them.
2. *Kids do their fair share of the work around here.* This gives kids an opportunity to feel a sense of importance to the family. (Listen to our audiotape titled *Chores* if there is any doubt about how to get the kids to do chores.)
3. *Don't cause a problem.* This means that if the kid causes a problem for the rest of the family, there will be appropriate consequences. If the child causes a problem for himself, the

parents will allow that problem to remain on the back of the child. Advice for solving the problem will be offered, and appropriate sadness will be expressed by the parents.

Responsibility for Meals

If I could raise my kids again, I'd have each one become responsible for one family meal per week. This would start when each child reached eight or nine years of age and would include planning, cooking, and serving the meal. Granted, this requires some training. However, this training time is quality time for both parents and kids and is soon offset by the amount of additional time parents will have for other activities as the years go on.

Kids who feel this responsibility and the resulting appreciation expressed by the parents have a special sense about their importance to the family and are far less likely to feel a need to join a gang. They have one at home.

• • •

I wish I had known these ideas when I was raising my children. Their lives and mine would have been better. However, I want you to know that my kids turned out great anyway, which shows how much kids can do for themselves. Kids are very resilient and adapt to a wide range of family and parenting styles as long as the parents are well meaning and loving.

© 1996 Jim Fay

CLINE'S CORNER

Abolishing Frustration
By Foster W. Cline, M.D.

VOL. 12, NO. 3

Hey, let's get real. Nothing takes away *all* the frustration from human relationships, and that includes raising children. But by gosh there are ways to avoid most of it and put more effective emotions in place.

As I said in a previous article, frustration is a poor emotion to emit to children because it both gives the children an emotion (which they love) and reveals the adult is out of control (which children, unfortunately, find absolutely irresistible).

There are only two main reason for chronic parental frustration.

The First Reason for Frustration

Parents become frustrated because they can't stop their children's self-destructive behavior. In fact, when parents get together in mutual wailing groups, they generally talk about their frustrations:

> "I can't make John quit making fun of other kids."
> "Robert wears the worst clothes to church."
> "Oh, I know, Paula has these cute little outfits that she refuses to wear."
> "Well, my problem with John is he's not going to have any friends."
> "Len is like that ... he's nasty to other kids sometimes. But he picks at his scabs—that drives me crazy."

Most of us parents love our children so much that it seems we can't help but be frustrated when they are doing something to mess up their lives. The problem is, frustration does *not* discourage but is *enjoyed* by the other guy!

What a bummer! If anyone should be unhappy over self-destructive behavior, it should be the person causing him/herself grief, right?

However, parents get caught being frustrated because sometimes the darn children refuse to be upset over the poor decisions they are making. But I have pretty good news. Generally,

1. if we come through *sad* that the child is making those decisions,
2. and don't rescue the child from the consequences—and hope the consequences cause some discomfort,
3. and set the example by taking care of ourselves,

our children will snap themselves around and stop the behavior that causes the frustration that worsens the behavior.

And I have more good news. If that doesn't work, getting frustrated is even less likely to help. So in almost all cases of self-destructive behavior the magic attitude is something along the lines of, "Gee, John, what a bummer for you! I bet you wonder sometimes if you're going to make it. Sometimes I wonder, too. It's kind of a sad situation for you, but if there was ever a kid who could probably turn it around, it's you."

The Second Reason for Frustration
Parents become frustrated because it takes so much psychic energy to fix the problems our kids cause themselves:

> "I have other things to do with my time than run to school bringing you your lunch!"
> "I just hate picking up after you when you make such a mess of your bathroom."
> "You know, it's expensive to keep paying for the orthodontic retainers you lose!"
> "I don't like having to talk to the other mothers about your behavior."
> "I have other things to do with my money than to pay for your lawyers, Troy."

More good news! If we want to be less frustrated, and the frustration is caused by an energy drain from rescuing the kids, then *stop it*. That's it, just stop it. No rescue, no frustration! (Then, you're not frustrated, but the kid is!)

Naturally, there are times children need rescue—and we covered that in the previous *Journal* article "Rules for Rescue" (Vol. 11, No. 4). But happily, the kids *usually* can cope with the consequences without rescue if we give them our concern, our care, our empathy, and our encouragement.

When rescuing parents quit the rescue, at first—but generally only at first—they may feel guilty and the kids may temporarily feel resentful:

MOM: "I guess you'll have to figure this one out, Joyce."

KID: "You mean you're not going to help me?"

MOM: "I don't think so this time, Honey. I decided I'm not going to drive back to the school to get things you forgot."

KID: "Don't you *love* me?"

(And the previously rescuing Mom wonders, looks pained, gets frustrated, and could still manage to mess up the situation.)

But sticking with it is the secret of doing away with 90 percent of the frustration of raising children. Substitute sorrow when they cause themselves problems, and either happily pull them out of the messes they get themselves into, or stop doing it so they can learn from their mistakes. Provide empathy, concern, and encouragement instead.

What a good deal. So much more satisfying than frustration!

© 1996 Foster W. Cline, M.D.

The Seeds of Happy Marriages Are Planted During Childhood
By Jim Fay
VOL. 12, NO. 4

There I was, doing one of my favorite things—hanging out in the supermarket watching kids and their parents. I get some of my best stories when I observe kids "putting their moves" on parents who are at high frustration levels trying to shop, stay within their budgets, and keep track of their kids.

Chris was systematically wearing his mother down. He was pushing a toy in her face, begging her to buy it, giving it his scatter-gun technique, trying anything that would make her feel guilty.

"But I really need this. Come on, Mom! It's only $7.95! You spent more than that on Carla last week. Why can't I have something for a change? I don't know why she always gets things and I don't. You like her better 'cause she's a girl. I never get anything. Please?"

Chris's mom finally lost the battle as well as her self-control. She was now screaming at him.

"Oh, all right! Put it in the cart! This is the last time you're going shopping with me. I don't know what's wrong with you. Why can't you leave me alone? Why do you always have to be so selfish? You don't need another toy. You never take care of the ones you have. All you can think of is more, more, more. You've got too much already!"

At this point, I stopped listening. It hurt too bad to hear the two of them going at each other, especially in light of my guess that this same scene will be played out almost every time the two of them go to the store together.

My heart goes out to Chris and his mom. I know that neither of them can be happy living out the interaction pattern they have developed together. Mom does not know how to set limits for Chris, so she screams insults at him, reminding him of his flaws every time she gets frustrated.

Chris is learning that criticizing and manipulating is the way to get what you want in life. As he grows older and looks for a mate, his selections are going to be limited. The emotionally healthy women won't be very interested in him, so he will have to choose from the pool of women who will play into his game.

Unfortunately, they will be like his mom, who screams and criticizes when things go wrong. He won't like that much and will probably end up with a low opinion of women. Of course, the emotionally healthy women he meets will tire of his game and drop him. The first rule of Love and Logic is "Take care of yourself in a very loving way." Love and Logic parents say this in several different ways:

- Set firm limits through enforceable statements.
- Tell your kids how you will take care of yourself instead of issuing orders.
- Never tell kids how to run their lives. Tell them how you are going to run yours. It is amazing what far-reaching implica-

tions are found in this rule, including implications that apply to Chris and his mother.

A Better Life for Chris

Think how much different Chris might be in the future and think how much different his eventual marriage might be if his mom practiced the rule "Take care of yourself." Let's run the tape backward and observe Mom taking care of herself instead of criticizing Chris:

CHRIS: "Mom, I need this."

MOM: "Do you have the money to buy it?"

CHRIS: "No. You buy it for me! It's not fair. Carla always gets stuff. I never get anything. She always gets her way 'cause you like her better. You're stupid."

MOM: "Chris, that was a really bad decision. I'm going to have to do something about that, but not here in public. I don't want to embarrass you in front of other people. I'll tell you at home. Try not to worry about it in the meantime. And, Sweetie, if it would help to throw a fit, feel free to do it on the sidewalk in front of the store. Come back in when you are sweet."

How is Mom taking care of herself?

1. She is not buying the toy.
2. She is not giving in to the manipulation and guilt.
3. She is not throwing an adult temper tantrum.
4. She is not trying to think up a consequence for Chris's misbehavior while trying to shop.
5. She is giving herself time to design an effective consequence.
6. She is giving herself time to get help from her friends, if necessary.
7. She is giving herself time to rehearse how she will deliver Chris's impending consequence.
8. She is not going to listen to Chris's temper tantrum.

9. She is allowing Chris's problem to remain his problem in a very loving way (the second rule of Love and Logic).
10. She is allowing Chris to learn that neither manipulation nor complaining are good ways to get what you want.

This Love and Logic mother will probably call Mabel, the baby-sitter that Chris hates. She'll ask Mabel to be Chris's sitter tomorrow morning. The next morning, mom will say to Chris, "I'm going shopping this morning. It's going to be a great day at the supermarket because you won't be there and I won't have to listen to begging and complaining. You will be hiring Mabel to take care of you. Ask her how much she is going to charge you. See you later, Sweetie."

How is Mom taking care of herself?

1. Chris is paying for the sitter.
2. Mom is not lecturing or threatening.
3. Mom will have a great time shopping on her own.
4. Mom is teaching Chris that her word is good. She will have fewer problems in the future.
5. Mom is finding out how easy it is to take care of herself compared to threatening, lecturing, screaming, and criticizing.
6. Mom is finding that a person can say, "Here is what I'm going to do" in a very soft voice and make it stick.
7. She is allowing Chris's problem to remain his problem in a very loving way (the second rule of Love and Logic).
8. She is giving Chris a chance to learn that manipulation and complaining don't work.

If Chris grows up in a home where Mom takes care of herself in a loving way, he will become conditioned to look for that kind of wife when he starts thinking about marriage. He will have learned a healthier way of interacting with women because of the good modeling his mother provided for him.

He will have a higher opinion of women and will probably treat them with more respect. The emotionally healthy women

KEN SCHULTZ'S

DAILY FISHING TIPS™

HOW TO CATCH MORE AND BIGGER FISH

A 2015 Full-Color Desk Calendar

GLADSTONE MEDIA
Keswick, Virginia

will be attracted to him and the odds go up for better relationships.

Unless Chris studies psychology, he may never know why he gets along so well in his marriage. It may not dawn on him that the seeds for his good relationships were planted during his early years by a mother who knew the importance of taking good care of herself in a very loving way.

© 1997 Jim Fay

In Defense of Consequences
By Foster W. Cline, M.D.
VOL. 12, No. 4

Those of us who are familiar with Love and Logic just naturally think in terms of consequences. We don't question their power or usefulness. We live and breathe consequences. But that's not true of everyone, even professionals.

Mark Mozei, Ph.D., of Helena, Montana, is one such professional. Under the heading "Kids Need Decisive Direction," he writes on the Internet:

The notion of natural consequences is a popular psychobabble concept. The theory is that one allows the kid's behavior to follow its naturally encountered, and the kid learns accordingly.

Two problems: (1) Natural consequences are generally delayed too long to have any effect. For example, when your dropout kid decides at age 25 that he shouldn't have blown off school, it's a little late to go back and do his seventh-grade homework.

Second, what really appeals to parents about natural consequences is that they're relieved of the unpleasant responsibility of coming down on the kid, and shaping him up. One can be indecisive, and cite "expert" opinion in support of not taking responsibility for the child's difficulties.

A particularly wacky rendition of the natural consequences idea is the "Good Luck" message, described in Parent Education Text *by Foster Cline, M.D. Dr. Cline cautions parents against ownership of problems that should rightfully be the child's and encourages parents to let their kids learn from the natural consequences of their own actions. However, parents can convey their concerns via a loving "Good Luck" message.*

Examples: "Cindy, with as much TV as you watch, I hope the old brain doesn't turn to squash. Good luck, Honey." Or, "Well, Robert, if you are going to head off to that party, from what I've heard of those kids, good luck!" And, "Well, Bobby, if that's the way your friends drive, and if you're going to keep riding with them, good luck!" (All from Cline; no, I didn't make this up.)

The doctor notes that the "Good Luck" message puts the problem on the kid's shoulders, and he starts to think, "I need more than luck! I better start thinking!" Yeah, riiight!

I'm really glad that the folks who write child-psych books obviously don't have kids. The world has enough goofy kids as it is. The "Good Luck" message makes sense, I guess, if you make the usual child-psych assumptions: (1) that raising kids is a mysterious psychological process, fraught with subtleties and nuances, (2) indirect, permissive strategies work best, allowing the kid to learn for himself, via natural consequences.

If you think your kid watches too much TV, there's a much simpler solution: Turn the stupid thing off and tell the kid to find something real to do. Likewise, if you think your kid is going to a booze party, or you're worried about the kids he rides with, don't wait until the "natural consequences" of a drinking problem or brain damage from a car wreck bring him around to your way of thinking: Put your foot down, just don't let him go.

Shazam! What a simple idea—you're the adult, don't make sarcastic hints, just take charge! In Nancy Reagan's immortal words, "Just say no!"

I guess Dr. Mozer publishes this public information without knowing any of our seven children, either the foster, adopted, or natural children. They're all grown now, doing great, and one, a Phi Beta Kappa and Fulbright scholar, would be happy to talk to Dr. Mozer about the power of consequences. Grandchildren are being raised with Love and Logic—exposed to natural and imposed consequences—and appear to be doing great.

But over and above the personal attacks, let's examine the meat of his thesis, that kids need direction, not consequences. Kids do need direction. That's obvious. I don't think anyone could argue with that; certainly Love and Logic does not.

But it is the *way* the direction is carried out that is so important. Actually, Love and Logic has no problem with giving certain kids, at certain times, orders, directions, and suggestions. There are numerous advantages:

1. Often it is the most expedient. (As Dr. Mozer notes, just say no and make 'em turn off that TV and stop drugs!)
2. The younger the child, the better it works.
3. It is very easy to do.
4. Sometimes it makes us feel good to tell them what they have to do.
5. "Decisive directions" are certainly one way of showing love.

But there are some other considerations:

1. Decisive directions are based on the assumption that I know more about the kid's situation than the kid. (Bill Gates dropped out of college to wire computers together in his garage. How do you think directive parents would have handled that?) Lots of problems over the years occur because

folks think they know better than another what's best for the other, and that includes parents.

2. Importantly, we can *always* give kids "decisive direction," suggestions, and orders, so let's not rush into it.

3. Most of the adult world, for which we are preparing our children, doesn't work on "decisive direction," but choices and consequences. Everyone has a right to be self-destructive, mess up his life, build on sand, not pay MasterCard, etc.

4. Decisive direction tends to be less effective with older kids. In fact, to use Dr. Mozer's example, "In Nancy Reagan's immortal words, 'Just say no!'" hasn't worked very well for America. And I will say from my experiences during thirty years in shrinkdom, a *lot* of drug-involved kids' parents decisively told them *not* to use drugs!

   Honestly, after raising all of our kids, and after working a professional lifetime with families, I'm a pretty pragmatic shrink. I don't think Dr. Mozer's ideas are wacky at all. If it works, do it. Rules and regulations are important, but in my experience, our kids respond best to "as few as possible, no more than necessary."

5. Finally, and this is the point of Love and Logic, "decisive direction" is not ideal for teaching kids how to think. Sure, making them turn off the TV is possible, and V-chips will work, but the problem is, when my kids are teens, none of their dates will come with V-chips. It will be up to my children to have *self*-discipline and to say *no to themselves.*

Do you want to buy into using consequences and having life's experiences help you out as your children learn, or would you rather be "decisively direct"? I believe the goal is to raise the best adults, not necessarily the best kids.

I'm happy to leave the choices and consequences to you.

© 1997 Foster W. Cline, M.D.

VOLUME

13

The Bad Report Card

By Jim Fay

VOL. 13, NO. 1

Jim, how do I react to my kid when he/she brings home a bad report card?

This is one of the most frequently asked questions I receive. The following is a sample letter a parent could write to the child as a way of responding effectively to this kind of problem.

The advantage of putting it in writing is that the youngster has an opportunity to get the parents' complete thoughts before having the opportunity to argue or defend. It usually works best to give the letter with a suggestion that the child think about it for a while before responding.

Dear Son,

Why do I want to know where you are and when you will be home?
Why do I expect you to respect me the way I respect you?
Why do I set expectations for school achievement?
Why do I expect you to do your share of the work around the house?
Why do I expect you at family meals?
Why do I set limits for you?

I do these things because it is the best way I know to prove to you that you are important to me and that I love you.

Having expectations for you is not easy. It makes a lot of extra work for me to hold you accountable. You test me frequently to see if I really do love you and believe in you.

You came home late to see what I would do, and you found that I limited your going out for a while. You talked back to me to see if I really loved you, and you ended up giving your sassy w̶ a lot of thought while you were doing some of my chores to̶ up for the energy drain you caused me.

You "forgot" to do your chores and were very surprised when I woke you up that night from a sound sleep to finish them. You tested me by being slow getting ready for school and missing the bus. What a long walk that was to school that day. You threw a fit one day at the shopping center and had to pay for a sitter the next time the rest of us went to the center.

Each time I laid down some consequences for you it broke my heart. I truly believe that it hurt me as much as it did you. And it was not easy to listen to you tell me that I did what I did because I was mean. Oh, how much easier it would have been to just yell at you, or spank you, or even excuse your behavior in some way. My love for you and my belief in what you can become were the only things that gave me the strength to do what I needed to do.

I know that adults who lead happy lives were once children who tested the limits of their parents and did not get their parents to wilt under the pressure. They grew up to be educated and responsible, and therefore equipped with what they needed to have the freedom to achieve their dreams.

I also know that the world is filled with people who did not have limits as children. You have seen these people yourself. The only life they will ever live is filled with disappointment.

Yesterday you brought home a report card with grades far below your ability level. It was only my tremendous belief in you that kept me from doing something we both might have regretted.

Please understand that it would be so much easier for me to make excuses for your behavior than to hold you accountable. It might even make me feel better if I could blame your poor grades on your age, your friends, or even your teacher.

But I love you too much to let you down that way.

Please give your school performance some serious thought and be ready to share your plans for solving this problem and getting your academic life back on track.

Your father and I will be available to discuss this with you on Friday evening. We want you to be prepared to tell us what you plan to do and also explain to us what kind of support or help you need from us.

I understand that you were hoping to go out Friday evening. Your father and I were planning to do the same. However, we are willing to stay home for this because you are so important to us and we care about the kind of person you become.

In the meantime, we understand you are probably hurting a great deal about your report card. It must be a great disappointment. Please tell your teachers you have our love and support.

Sincerely,
Mom

There are several advantages to approaching the problem in this manner. First of all, it gives both the parents and the child time to cool down and put the situation into proper perspective. It gives the parents time to consult with teachers and counselors.

This approach also gives the parents time to rehearse how they want to come across to the youngster when they finally meet on the subject, and greatly reduces the emotions and power struggle aspects of the problem.

An important factor in dealing with a problem in this manner is that the child gets to learn, first of all, that the parents' love and support are the most important issues at hand. Warnings, threats, and arguments often cause both parents and child to forget their love and commitment to each other.

© 1997 Jim Fay

CLINE'S CORNER

The Misuse of Love and Logic
By Foster W. Cline, M.D.

Vol. 13, No. 1

Love and Logic is built on three basic principles. After making sure the child has been given the correct information in an age-appropriate and loving manner, Love and Logic parents:

1. Separate the problem.
2. Give choices for a solution.
3. Let the consequences for the decision flow unhindered by parental protection.

There are three common parental mistakes that can make each of these principles less effective. I am reminded of this when, so often, parents almost gleefully tell me how much their kids hate Love and Logic (only at first, I hope).

Really, the idea is to empower the kids in such a way that they appreciate the Love and Logic principles as much as their parents do—the sooner the better. Let's look at the three unnecessary reasons why kids may feel uncomfortable, if not downright nasty, about Love and Logic.

Reason 1 for Kid Upset: The parents have—and display—too much joy in laying the child's problem on the child.
Many parents, when first introduced to Love and Logic, burn themselves out worrying about their children's problems. This is particularly sad when it's only one child! But overprotective parents get mired down in taking care of their children's problems: rescuing them, warning them, haranguing them, and punishing them for the problems they bring on themselves, etc., etc. Most of you know the routine!

When first encountering Love and Logic, it is like a breath of fresh air to these parents: "Wow, you mean I don't have to be concerned about all my kid's problems? I thought being a good parent was making school visits, warning, worrying and rescuing, and making sure they straightened themselves out. This is *freedom*!"

Because Love and Logic places the burden of responsibility for behavior and the consequences of that directly on the child, the parents, now relatively unburdened, practically rub their hands in glee: "I can't wait to try this on my kid!" We hear this at workshops over and over.

While such glee is understandable, it is not necessarily helpful to the child who will be *suffering* the consequences of his or her poor decisions. The child will, as many Americans do now, resent taking care of himself when somebody else has heretofore been attempting to ensure his health and happiness. (One mother said, "I have been the welfare system! No wonder I've run out of patience, money, and energy while the kid is getting worse!")

Understandably but incorrectly, then, the parents show downright joy when they say to their startled offspring, "That's your problem, you'll have to take care of it."

It is best for the parents to talk about their new way of thinking and behaving. Let the child know why this will be good for him or her in the long run, if painful in the short run. Then, when parents lay the problem on their child, it must be done softly, and with affection, while still giving the message, "If anyone can handle it, it's you, Sweetie."

Reason 2 for Kid Upset: The parents misuse choices by arranging a punishment in the area of the child's problem.
Once parents understand the power of choices—paradoxically, power given, by power given away—they often tend to give artificial choices (read punishment) in areas that are really the child's business. This was best exemplified by a mother who thanked me for making her life so much easier, and stated, "Now I give the kids choices. Are they going to choose to wear their shoes when they play in the snow or are they going to go barefoot and then choose to miss dinner?"

Over the years, I have seen many parents misuse choices by providing a choice of punishment in the child's area of concern. Remember, mainly choices are given so the child will be aware of *natural* consequences of their actions, or to take care of ourselves by telling the kids what we are willing to do in certain circumstances.

Reason 3 for Kid Upset: Parents refuse to ever rescue.
When first learning of Love and Logic, rescuing parents, suddenly feeling set free, take nonrescue to the extreme. (This situation can be avoided if parents follow the Love and Logic "Rules for Rescue" in Vol. 11, No. 4, of the *Love and Logic Journal*.)

The reason for uncertainty about who and when to help is culturally induced by the media, which talk about "corporate welfare" as if it can be compared to the usual welfare handout.

Now, it may be that government help for corporations should be less; it probably should be. But it is disingenuous to call it "corporate welfare." For in the case of corporations, the government is helping out an entity that is working hard. The corporation is asking for help to have an advantage in the workplace. It wants to do what it does, only more so.

Equating corporate welfare with the average welfare handout is like equating the parental help given a high-achieving child who asks the parents for money to go to college with the son who, on drugs, wants the parents to pay for his habit and provide room and board.

Wise Love and Logic parents will always help the first child, who will scale even greater heights. Unwise parents who provide money in the second example will see their son sink to even greater depths.

So it's okay to rescue your child and pull him or her out of some jam if:

1. The child can learn from the experience despite the lessened suffering your rescue provides.
2. The child is honestly appreciative and doesn't feel entitled to the help.
3. The child generally does not need this type of rescue, so you are not enabling a chronically dysfunctional lifestyle.

Once parents, like the government, help people who feel entitled to receive help in support of their chronically poor choices and painful lifestyles, then all hope for growth and change is lost.

© 1997 Foster W. Cline, M.D.

"Don't Slam the Door!"
By Jim Fay

VOL. 13, No. 2

"Jim, I've got to tell you about this," said one of the participants in a recent Love and Logic seminar. She excitedly went on to say, "I finally got to my teen. He would never listen to me. I must have told him a thousand times not to slam the door when he gets mad, but he goes deaf every time I open my mouth."

As she talked, it occurred to me that her success came when she quit telling him what to do and allowed him to learn from experience. She did what good Love and Logic parents do. She gave good advice and allowed her son to decide for himself whether to take her advice.

All this happened the following way. During a rare good moment with her son, she commented, "Jeremy, do you realize that slamming the door could cause the window to break? You might want to give that some thought."

Jeremy's reaction was, "Jeez, Mom. You worry about everything. Besides, why can't you ever stand to see me express my feelings? I'm supposed to go around here pretending that everything is perfect all the time. Am I supposed to stuff all my feelings? Jeez!"

No more was said. The subject was dropped. However, it wasn't long before Jeremy's temper got the better of him. Jeremy and his mother had a disagreement. He wanted more allowance and his mom told him that if he needed more money, he was going to have to do more chores around the house or find a part-time job.

Jeremy was furious. "Fine! Just fine! I didn't ask to be born into a family with tightwad parents. None of my friends have to put up with this. You guys only had kids so you could make slaves out of them. I'm out of here. I don't have to put up with doing all of your work!"

He ran to the front door, jerked it open, and screamed, "I hate you!" He then slammed the door with all of his might. The next sound was that of shattering glass as the window broke.

Buy Yourself Some Time

Jeremy was gone for three hours. This gave Mom time to call some of her friends to get some advice. One of her friends had studied the book *Parenting with Love and Logic*. She made some suggestions. Her first suggestion was that Mom buy herself more time to think out a plan. She could do this by telling Jeremy she was going to do something about the broken window, but not immediately. She was first going to talk with all her friends and get some ideas.

The second suggestion her friend gave her was to say to Jeremy, "Try not to worry about it in the meantime." This would more than likely cause Jeremy to worry a lot more than usual.

When a Kid Makes a Problem, Allow the Problem to Remain His Problem

Mom's friend also reminded her of the rule in Love and Logic that says, "When a kid makes a problem, allow the problem to remain the kid's problem. Do this in a loving way with no anger, lectures, threats, or warnings."

Mom Is Now in the "Driver's Seat"

When Jeremy came home, his mother met him at the door with, "Jeremy, I'm really sorry your door-slamming turned out so bad for you. I called the glass company and had them put that plywood over the window for now. I'm going to have to do something about this later, but we both need at least one good night's sleep before we discuss it. Actually, it may take me a few days to decide. I want to call my friends and get some ideas first. In the meantime, try not to worry too much about what's going to happen."

"Wait a minute, here. What are you pulling? How come you're acting so nice? What are you up to? Come on. Tell me. What are you going to do?"

"Not now," said Mom. "I've got to give this a lot of thought. Try not to worry about it. I'll talk to you later." She walked off grinning to herself.

Before You Act, Make Your Plan and Practice Your Delivery

Two days later Mom talked with Jeremy. "I know you've been worried about the window. It's going to have to be replaced. Here's the phone number of the glass company that put the plywood on the door. The manager is expecting you to call and arrange for him to finish the job and tell him how you plan to make payment."

"I'm not paying for that stinkin' window. It's your fault. You made me mad!"

Mom had learned from her friend how to handle the backtalk. Mom's friend showed her a list of Love and Logic "One-Liners for Backtalk" found in the *Love and Logic Catalog*. Armed with this strategy, Mom calmly replied, "Don't worry about it now. We'll talk about it later."

As he continued to argue, Mom calmly repeated the same thing, "Don't worry about it now, we'll talk about it later." She then added, "There's no hurry to have the job done and paid for. Just have it done before you drive the family car again. I'll take your keys, thank you."

Jeremy was mad, but he had no choice other than to arrange for the repair. He had to find some odd jobs with the neighbors to make payment. Mom was smart enough not to bring up the subject again other than to thank him for getting the job done.

The Lesson Learned

One week later Jeremy witnessed an argument brewing between his mother and his younger brother. As the argument became more heated, he heard the brother say, "I'm out of here!" as he headed for the front door.

It was at this point that Mom realized Jeremy was screaming to his brother at the top of his lungs, *"Don't slam the door!"*

© 1997 Jim Fay

Friends

By Jim Fay and Foster Cline

VOL. 13, NO. 2

Friends. From the time our kids get off the knees of infancy and onto the land legs of toddlerhood, they're going to be around other kids. Playing with dolls. Shooting baskets. Swapping baseball cards. Running in the neighborhood.

Our kids are going to make friends. That's the good news. As we know, friends are great for kids to have. The bad news is that often we don't like the friends they choose.

One of the biggest mistakes we parents make is getting into a control battle with our kids over who their friends are. We'll lose that one every time. Since we can't win that battle, we should keep our mouths shut and take a different track. We should concentrate on the areas we can control.

We can offer our kids a choice: Pick friends we approve of and then play with those friends at our house, or pick friends we don't approve of and then make sure they never come near the house. Or we can say, "Would you like to have friends who really test your decision-making and thinking skills, or would you rather have some who don't pressure you so much?"

The key relationship in discussing our kids' friendships with them is the one between us and our kids. That must be preserved. When we try to change our kids' relationships, it may damage our own relationship with our children. Our kids rebel against our demands and orders.

Prohibiting our kids from playing with certain friends tells them we are afraid the friends' attitudes, beliefs, or habits will rub off. It also tells our kids they can't do their own thinking. The result is usually that the friends become more exciting and desirable.

But we can tell them what we think. Children cannot rebel against thoughts and opinions. In fact, if our relationship with our kids remains communicative, in the long run our kids will generally pick friends we like.

Joan is about to leave the house for a rendezvous with friends of hers whom her father doesn't approve of:

JOAN: "Hey, Dad, I'm leaving."

DAD: "Wait a minute. Let's have a good-bye hug."

JOAN: "Oh ... Okay."

DAD: "Are you going out with Jean and Debby?"

JOAN: "Yeah ... so?"

DAD: "So ... great! I'm just hoping, Dear, that some of you rubs off on them."

JOAN: "Oh, Dad."

DAD: "Honey, I'm serious. Sometimes I think those kids need you around them. Maybe you're a good influence on them or something."

JOAN: "You don't like them."

DAD: "It's not a matter of not liking them, Joan. I just worry sometimes that life may not go as smoothly for those kids as I hope yours goes for you. Now, run along and have a good time."

We may be pleasantly surprised when we get to know our children's friends. Our kids often see good in others that we simply don't see. When we get to know our kids' friends, we may get to know more about our kids, too. We may understand why they're attracted to certain people.

From the book Parenting with Love and Logic:
Teaching Children Responsibility.
© *1990 Foster W. Cline, M.D., and Jim Fay*

CLINE'S CORNER

Handling Peer Pressure
By Foster W. Cline, M.D.

Vol. 13, No. 2

My child is in fourth grade and now is starting to worry about what other kids think of the way he dresses. In third grade he was willing to be different. It seems he is regressing. What do I do?

Two facts about peer pressure to help put things in perspective. First, peer pressure is universal. The adult word for *peer pressure* is "status."

Haven't we all seen women carrying a shoddily made, brown, fake-leather handbag, with tan manufacturer's initials all over it? Most of these ladies have paid more for this cheaply made merchandise because it is a status symbol.

Watches that keep poorer time than an inexpensive Casio sell for thousands of dollars because they are status symbols. Some people even buy vehicles with the make of the vehicle splashed across the side of the car. They are essentially moving billboards for the manufacturer. Yet people buy these items because they are status symbols.

Chic clothes designers count on peer pressure and status to sell clothing that, really, no one would be caught dead in if it were bought at J.C. Penney. It's considered great only because it was created by a certain costly French designer.

That's peer pressure. Children and adults are both equally susceptible to it.

Second, peer pressure in childhood is a normal developmental stage. Kids are particularly susceptible in their eighth through fourteenth years. (Although, as noted above, some adults never outgrow their need to respond to peer pressure.)

At these ages there is a developmental feeling among all children that "Different is bad." Every kid is developmentally saying,

"I am a child not only of my family, but also of my group of friends, and my standing in the group is important to me."

Every teacher during these years attempts to get kids to celebrate differences. And as soon as the kids are in the mall, they start making fun of others outside their "in group." The need for group identity is so strong that some schools require uniforms as a discipline technique.

Children in elementary school have a hard time identifying with the abstract value systems of other children and friends. No kid comes home and says, "I run with a group that has the basic work ethic" or "I fit in with middle-class, low-achieving kids."

Instead, children begin to find their identity outside the family by identifying with the concrete issue of apparel and "special behavior," be it simply different or antisocial. Most of this human developmental need to look similar to others in the group starts in late elementary school, and continues on through adulthood.

There are answers for dealing with the peer pressure your child experiences. First, what not to do.

If the child's peer beliefs go against your own home's belief system, don't support them, but don't deride the peer beliefs, either. It is possible to not support an issue without saying, "That music has no redeeming qualities," "Tattoos are stupid," or "I think that looks dumb." The need for certain brands of clothes or specific types of music can be questioned without being put down.

The issue of quality and value can be talked about, but ultimately, it is not helpful to deny completely what peers think is important. If peer pressure leads the child into self-destructive behavior, don't rescue your child, and make sure he or she knows you will not rescue them.

Children who know they must face the consequences of their decisions tend to give decisions more thought than children who know their parents will simply become angry and then rescue them.

Second, the answer for parents is not to try to stop a child's susceptibility to peer pressure, but instead to provide wise counseling about it. Early on, it is generally enough to encourage your child to internally question the value of what peers are doing without requiring that he or she go directly against the peer belief.

It's okay to say we see things differently. And if the kids want "the best" skis and the most expensive clothes, it is a good idea to ask them to pay the difference between the good stuff and the expensive items the children think they have to have ... and you save your money for the Lexus!

Unless something is really important, Love and Logic dictates that parents allow the child to make mistakes and learn from the consequences:

DAD: "Honey, you want a tattoo?"

KID: "Yeah, Dad, I do."

DAD: "Why?"

KID: "I think it looks neat."

DAD: "I think you have a great body just the way God colored it."

KID: "Dad, everyone has a tattoo."

DAD: "Everyone?"

KID: "Well, not everyone, but I want one."

DAD: "Darlin', I wish you wouldn't, and I hope you give it lots of thought. Whatever it is, I hope your future spouse will think it's great, too. And your kids. Good luck!"

One adolescent rightly noted, "Mom, if getting a little tattoo on my back is the worst thing I ever do, you are in fat city."

"Can't I Just Have a Spanking, *Please*?"
By Jim Fay
VOL. 13, NO. 3

I've been around so long and have given so many presentations and interviews that I never have to be lonely in the airport anymore. There is always someone around who recognizes me and wants to tell me stories about their use of Love and Logic.

I often hear parents telling me their kids would much rather have a spanking than to have Love and Logic used on them. Several parents have even said that their kids have asked, "Why can't you just spank me like other parents?"

I spotted a couple in Denver International Airport recently. It was evident that they recognized me, so I went over to them. They were saying, "We hope we aren't bothering you, but we recognized you from videos we have been studying. We have been taking the course 'Become a Love and Logic Parent.' It was so much fun for us and we learned so much that we could use right away. Can we tell you a story?"

They went on to tell how they had tried out a technique designed to tell when a child is old enough to take on new opportunities or responsibilities. This technique involves asking the youngster how he or she plans to handle peer pressure or temptations.

"Our fourteen-year-old daughter wanted to go out with some older kids who had a car. So we asked her if there might be drugs or alcohol there. She told us, 'Of course, they're everywhere. It's no big deal.'"

Her parents had learned to ask how she planned on handling kids pushing drugs or alcohol on her and were aware that if she responded with answers like "I just say no," "I tell them it's stupid," or "You know I don't do those things," that she was still not mature enough to handle the pressures.

However, the daughter said, "That happens all the time. It's really no problem. I just tell the kids that I like them and want to do stuff with them, but I'm really not into that scene, but thanks anyway."

Her parents were impressed with her maturity and suggested that she go and have a good time, but that she was expected home by 10:00. As you might guess, she was not home by 10:00, but at 10:15 the parents got a frantic call: "I'm sorry, I know I'm late. The driver took us over on the other side of town. I thought I better call because I knew that you'd be worried. I'm really sorry, but it's not my fault!"

Dad responded with, "That was good of you to call. We were starting to worry. Where are you right now?"

"We're at the 7-Eleven store out on Highway 53."

"Great. I know where that is. Tell your friends to wait with you there and I will come and get you."

Dad heard her turn to the kids and tell them that her dad was coming to get her. At the same time he heard one of the girls in the background getting upset and yelling, "Oh great! He's going to come over here and start yelling at us and then you're going to get grounded!"

Dad also heard his daughter trying to calm her friend down with, "Wait a minute. My dad doesn't yell and scream and ground me. He uses Love and Logic."

This is the point at which the daughter's friend really lost control. She started screaming all the more, "Oh, geez! I'd rather get screamed at and grounded!"

This story is typical of many I hear about kids who'd rather be punished with old, more traditional ways than have to live with the consequences of their bad decisions.

In the past many childhood misbehaviors were handled with spanking or grounding. Now that experts know more about kids and especially now that the Love and Logic techniques have been developed and refined, there is no need for these kinds of punishments, especially spanking.

The position we outlined in our book *Parenting with Love and Logic* was our thinking as of 1990, when the book was written. Since then our knowledge has grown. The world we live in has changed, and we have developed new and additional techniques that are far more effective than spanking.

For the record, the Love and Logic Institute's present position on spanking is:

1. There is no need for spanking. Spanking is not as effective as many Love and Logic techniques.
2. Research now shows that spanking has quick results but actually makes the problem worse in the long run.

3. Spanking is counterproductive. It lets the kid "off the hook" and makes the adult into the bad guy in the child's mind.
4. Kids who are spanked develop long-term resentment toward adults.
5. Love and Logic techniques are far more powerful.
6. Most kids would much rather have a spanking than have their parents use Love and Logic techniques such as delaying the consequence while the parent thinks over the problem, develops a clear head, and then locks in the empathy before telling the child what the consequence will be.
7. Since we now have such better techniques, why even consider spanking a kid?

© 1997 Jim Fay

A Phone Call from the Police
By Charles Fay, Ph.D.
VOL. 13, No. 3

The phone rang at 1 a.m. It was the police informing my friend that her fifteen-year-old son had just been arrested for shoplifting. The officer continued, "... and we also found a bag of marijuana in his backpack."

How might a parent respond to this type of phone call? In my travels around the country, parents often provide similar examples and ask, "What in the world should I do?" Grappling for answers to their questions, I've found help in the two basic rules of Love and Logic:

1. Parents take good care of themselves by setting limits in a loving way.
2. Parents help their children learn valuable life lessons by replacing punishment with empathy and logical consequences.

How do Love and Logic rules apply to very serious issues such as drug use, violations of the law, violent behavior, etc.? As a psychologist working with these sorts of problems, I've observed that successful parents do four things when their teens violate the law:

1. They find a way to place the problem on the teen's shoulders rather than their own, and they do not rescue their child from legal consequences.
2. They set limits only on issues they can actually control.
3. They set limits primarily with actions rather than words.
4. They maintain these limits by replacing lecturing and arguing with empathy and calm persistence.

How did my friend place her son's shoplifting and drug possession charges squarely yet gently upon his shoulders, rather than her own? She didn't act like a Helicopter parent, who would have shown up at the police station in her night robe yelling, "You've made a big mistake here, Mr. Police Officer. My Johnny is incapable of doing something like this! You'll be hearing from our lawyer!"

She also didn't act very much like a Drill Sergeant parent, arriving at the station yelling, "Son, how many times have I told you to be responsible?! You really screwed up this time! You are never leaving the house again and I mean it!"

As she heard the officer speak to her over the phone, and after she started to calm down from the initial shock, my friend kept saying to herself, "Take care of yourself ... logical consequences plus empathy ... take care of yourself ... logical consequences plus empathy."

This was her way of staying calm and remembering the two basic rules of Love and Logic. Next, she thought to herself, "Do I want my son to do this again? No! Will the consequences of this behavior be more affordable now or when he is twenty? Now! Will he learn wisdom from this mistake? Only if I stay calm, show him empathy, and don't rescue him!"

Here's how she responded to the officer:

OFFICER: "Come down here and get him as soon as you can!"
MOM: "I'm really confused."
OFFICER: "What's the problem? Why are you confused?"

Mom: "What will it teach my son if I come and get him right away?"

Officer: "What are you talking about?"

Mom: "Well, do you want my son down there more often?"

Officer: "What are you talking about, Ma'am?"

Mom: "Would it be possible to keep him locked up until morning? I mean so that he will learn a good lesson from this and not hassle you in the future."

Officer: "We need you to come down and get him tonight."

Mom: "This is really unfortunate ... and there's another problem. I'll need to find a way to get down there from here."

Officer: "We need you down here as soon as possible."

Mom: "I'm so upset I'm not sure I'm safe to drive. I'll need to call a friend."

Officer: "Okay, be here as soon as possible."

This was a tough conversation for Mom! Unfortunately, she and the police officer didn't see eye-to-eye on what should be done. Her only option was to take some time to calm down, think about a plan, and call a friend to drive her to the station. By the time she arrived at the station it was already 6:30 a.m.

Rather than rescuing, yelling, or screaming, my friend took good care of herself by getting calmed down and waiting until a reasonable time the next morning to visit the police station. By resisting her urge to run down to the station at 1 a.m., and to yell, scream, and eventually rescue her son, she communicated to him that she would not be owning his problem.

And do you suppose this little bit of extra jail time might have been a good way of teaching her son some real-world wisdom? Probably so!

Now came the hard part. My friend anticipated the pain of talking with her son as she drove to the station. As she sat down with him and the police officer, she kept reminding herself over and over, "Keep it his problem, set a controllable limit, avoid arguing!" Here's how the conversation sounded:

MOM:	"I'm glad you're okay. I was really worried."
SON:	"Where were you? What took you so long to get down here?"
MOM:	"I wanted to be fair and respectful to you. I was too upset to drive. I needed to find someone to drive me here."
SON:	"You know what happened, don't you?"
MOM:	"Yes. This is so sad."
SON:	"What?"
MOM:	"This is so sad. What are you going to do?"
SON:	"Don't know—maybe I need a lawyer?"
MOM:	"Maybe. Have you thought about how you might get one?"
SON:	"No ... don't know."
MOM:	"That's sad."
SON:	"Maybe you can get me one?"
MOM:	"Oh, I'm sorry. Would I ask you to get me a lawyer if I was in trouble?"
SON:	"You can't do this! Dad would have helped me! You don't love me!"
MOM:	"You're mad."
SON:	"What do you expect me to do?"
MOM:	"I don't know. I've never been in your spot."
SON:	"What kinda mom are you anyway?"
MOM:	"You're really mad."
SON:	"So what am I supposed to do?"
MOM:	"Would you like some ideas?"
SON:	"Okay."
MOM:	"Some kids look through the phone book for free or low-cost legal advice. How would that work for you?"
SON:	"Okay, I guess I'll try it ... but why can't you just help me get a lawyer?"
MOM:	"What did I say about that?"

This was an even tougher conversation for Mom! Nevertheless, she was eventually successful in getting her son to find and pay for his own legal help. The key to her success was in:

1. Keeping the problem on her son's shoulders.
2. Setting limits on matters she could control (such as when she would drive to the police station and whether she would get him a lawyer).
3. Setting limits with actions rather than just words (such as taking her time getting to the station and refusing to give in despite his manipulation).
4. Maintaining the limits she set by remaining calm, using empathy, and refusing to argue.

The worst thing she could have done for her son would have been to scream and yell and get him a lawyer. Instead, she gave him something much more important. She allowed him to learn a wise lesson about how choices affect one's life—a lesson better learned as a teenager than as an adult.

© 1997 Charles Fay, Ph.D.

CLINE'S CORNER

Gifts: Helping Kids Be More Appreciative
By Foster W. Cline, M.D.
VOL. 13, NO. 3

Present time. It is almost that time of year. Although most of us stress the importance of teaching our children the real meaning of the holidays, and how unimportant the trappings, tinsel, and gifts are, children's little brains are still synapsing about presents. That's pretty normal.

"What did you bring me?"
"Hers is bigger than mine."

And the parents wonder:

"Can I get Troy one without getting Jason one too?"
"Honey, don't you think we've bought the kids enough?"

The holidays. Giving, receiving, presents, and joy all go together—usually. And although the "holiday blues" are common ("Shouldn't I be a lot happier right now?"), most people are giving and receiving gifts.

Many parents will be raining fits on their kids. In too many homes, opening gifts is a self-indulgent orgy in which the child goes from ripping the paper off one present, looking at the present long enough for one adult to open one present, and then ripping open the next.

There are some Love and Logic rules for giving presents that wise parents follow:

Guideline 1: If your kid is unappreciative of gifts, give less.

If your kid is bored, unappreciative, or not pleasantly responsive when receiving a gift, there is a good chance that you are raising an entitled brat. The kid is simply getting and expecting too much.

As the song "Santa Claus Is Coming to Town" warns, "You better watch out, you better not cry; Better not pout, I'm telling you why ... He's making a list and checking it twice; Gonna find out who's naughty and nice ..."

Too many of today's kids honestly think pouting and being naughty or nice have nothing to do with whether they get their stash during the holidays. It's somehow owed to them.

Guideline 2: All kids should be equally loved and equally treated.

Robert and Jan were stepparents. They had his, her, and their kids. Jan's parents showered expensive gifts only on the children of her first marriage. In fact, I have found it is not uncommon for grand-parents to play favorites. Some kids get too much from them and others get little or nothing.

Jan handled the situation magnificently: "Mom, Paul's joy at getting your gifts at Christmas doesn't outweigh the disappoint-ment of the other children who get little or nothing form you. So, since our family is basically into feeling as joyful as possible at Christmas, I won't be giving your gifts to Paul."

Guideline 3: Equal treatment does not always mean equal gifts.
The happiest parents know there are different strokes for different folks. That's the way the world works. Sometimes one kid needs something expensive. The other kid doesn't.

As long as sometimes one kid gets something needed and expensive and sometimes the others do, it is safe to give unequal gifts. Parents who equally love their kids, and are equally generous overall, don't have to feel like they need to give equal-value gifts on every occasion.

Guideline 4: You don't have to buy into marketing hype.
By the time the holidays roll around, your kids have been bombarded with advertising pitches. They want a "look-like-me doll," or a particular game. Nothing else will do. They know what they want.

Sometimes it is okay to gratify such whims. What the child wants and what's been advertised is really pretty neat. At other times you are just falling for Madison Avenue's pitch.

It's perfectly okay to say to a child, "Honey, buying stuff like that simply does not fit my value system. It's not what I do. But I can understand your wanting it. For heaven's sake, buy it!"

Guideline 5: Be creative about opening gifts.
No need to necessarily open all twenty gifts within a twelve-hour period. One family felt it was much more meaningful to the children when the gifts were opened over a period of "the twelve days of Christmas."

And as most people know, this is a Hanukkah tradition. The dad told me, "We let the kids pick which gift they want to open on which day, and they look forward to each gift." The parents felt this approach definitely increased the meaningfulness of the gift.

Guideline 6: Teach your child the joy of giving.
The joy of giving more than matches the joy of receiving. Teach your children this. Some of them may not come by it naturally. Show your enthusiasm about giving to others and it will be contagious: "Wow,

I bet when we take this turkey over to the Salvation Army, they will be so happy. I bet this will bring big smiles to their faces!"

Or, "I know it is so hard to pick things out for your brother. But you always seem to light up his life with what you pick. I can hardly wait to be surprised and see what you've chosen this year."

The value of giving gifts is only meaningful if the children spend their own money. This means many kids are very creative about what they make for gifts. And gifts that a child makes tend to be more exciting and gratifying than what they buy. So emphasize the real meaning of the holidays. Keep the children in touch with why we are celebrating, and handle the present situation so it's more gratifying and fun for everyone.

© 1997 Foster W. Cline, M.D.

Skipping School
By Jim Fay
Vol. 13, No. 4

Jim, what am I going to do with my high school daughter? I just got a call from the school and discovered she has been going to school and then leaving. She's not attending classes. I don't know where she is going or how she is using her time. She's even been intercepting the messages from school on the answering machine, so I didn't know the problem was going on. I'm at my wit's end with this kid! I just knew her friends were going to get her into trouble!

As a parent it's easy and natural to blame problems on the kids our teens hang out with. But let's be careful about that. The problem usually goes deeper than this. We are going to need to look a lot more closely to find the real causes of this youngster's problems with school.

Before we blame the friends, it's helpful to remember that she picks friends who meet her needs and won't make her feel out of place.

The solution for skipping school is complicated. It often requires a shift of the parent–child relationship and a clear picture of why the streets appear safer to the child than being in school. We need to get a picture of how she sees herself in relationship to achieving with school tasks.

There are questions regarding her relationship with the parents as well as how she feels about her teachers. Does she feel that her basic needs for affection, control, inclusion, and competence are being met?

After forty-three years of working with kids and families, I know what will make it worse. Anger, lectures, warnings, threats, and grounding are typical parental reactions that do nothing but create a bigger rift between parent and child.

The best odds for success come when parents work with their kids through genuine concern and a sincere desire to help make things better, rather than through anger and punishment. (Please don't confuse this with letting the teen off the hook. She must face up to the problem she is causing for others.)

I'd suggest the parents *start* by writing a letter to their teen as follows:

Dear Daughter,

We are writing to you at this time because we want you to give this letter some thought before you answer.

This is a sad situation. We are concerned for you and want to help. We are writing to you so you will understand that we don't want to fall into the trap of anger, arguing, threatening, lecturing, and warning, because these actions will only make things worse for all of us.

Some kids do what you did because of a school problem. Some do it because of other kid problems. Some do it because they have a problem with their parents, and some do it for kicks and then realize it wasn't right. I hope you will give this some thought and let us know so we can work with you and give you the support that you need to get through this.

Please understand that as parents we have a responsibility to you to help you learn as much as possible about the real world, by helping you live with your bad decisions so your future decisions will be better thought-out.

We will need to come up with a consequence that is fair to all of us, so we won't be able to tell you right away what it is. We will give it a lot of thought and then let you know.

In the meantime, please know that we love you very much and understand that you are going through a lot of pain right now. It is during times such as these that we are reminded that the most valuable thing we all have is our relationship.

Love,
Mom and Dad

One suitable consequence would be to have the teen do enough chores to pay back for the time and energy the parents devote to dealing with this problem. If you have trouble getting kids to do their chores, refer to our audiotape *"Didn't I Tell You to Take Out the Trash?"*

Parents of very resistive kids have the kids pay someone to supervise the chores so they get them done. They tell their kids they love them too much to fight with them about the chores. This may give the teen a chance to learn about garage sales or the use of pawn shops.

The ultimate solution will surface when the teen feels very loved and invested in the home and the school. Ways of doing this include two basic strategies.

First, parents and teachers replace guiltful, angry, and lecturing words with loving comments such as, "We miss you when you are gone" and "I get scared when I don't know where you are."

Second, parents and teachers ask the teen to help them create a better home and classroom environment. This involves having the teen do important jobs such as preparing at least one family meal per week. This is not punishment, but a chance for her to feel important and valued as a family member.

The school can help by creating plans for improving the relationship the teen has with her teachers. Specific techniques for developing better teacher–pupil relationships can be found in the first few chapters of *Teaching with Love and Logic.*

This is also a good time to seek the help of a good therapist or counselor who approaches the problem by working with the parents, child, and school, not just the child. If the teen won't go to therapy, don't give up. The parent works with the therapist and the school to encourage the teen rather than threaten them.

Once a threat or power struggle is in place, the teen often gets in a way of thinking that says, "I'd rather die than allow my parents and the school to win." This doesn't need to happen. Most kids respond to our genuine concern and love better than they do to our threats and warnings.

© 1998 Jim Fay

CLINE'S CORNER

What Motivates Kids to Excel?
By Foster W. Cline, M.D.
Vol. 13, No. 4

Question

There is a debate in my state about standards-based education. My son seems to feel that just meeting the standard is all he wants to do. And we've had to take away many privileges to get him to do his work. Do standards encourage mediocrity?

Is it right to take away extracurricular activities like gymnastics and soccer when the schoolwork isn't done? The consequences imposed at school—bad grades and staying in from recess to finish work—aren't enough to motivate him. All his grades aren't bad, but his lack of interest in doing well bothers me.

Answer

There are more than a dozen reasons for underachievement. Some of these reasons, of course, have numerous subcategories. There are genetic, birth, neurological, and many psychological reasons for underachievement. I started to list all of the reasons for under-achievement, and I realized that would take up all the space we have for the entire article!

Not to fear! Love and Logic tools work for almost all situations, so parents don't have to become diagnosticians. Love and Logic tools don't neglect the problem if it is neurological and correctable, and won't heighten the rebellion if the problem is psychological.

Whether the problem is a learning deficit, or the more common learning lag, Love and Logic tools help ensure the problem is not worsening by the way parents handle it.

Following are the main rules for underachieving children:

- Make sure that as a parent, you do as little as possible to own the problem. Whether the problems are psychological or neuro-logical, they belong to the child. "Too bad *you* have this prob-lem, Honey, it must make it difficult for you at times."

  Parents certainly need to help children with ADD and other problems get organized; yet the correct parenting attitude is, "I really want to do as little as possible to take care of your prob-lem so you learn how to handle it yourself."
- Make sure you talk with teachers and other professionals. Never be afraid of the school providing your child the testing needed to get to the bottom of the problem. Get an outside opinion if you don't like the school's conclusion.
- If the problem is neurological, a learning problem, or other medical issue, an overlay of psychological negativism is gener-ally present—none of us like being forced to perform in our area of weakness. Because of the negative attitude, it is easy to lose sight of the deeper issue.
- Of the neurological, ADD, learning disorder group, many prob-lems are outgrown. Others remain for a lifetime. But in *either*

case, the parent is safest in giving encouragement and love, and in allowing the *natural* consequences to take place.

Remember, the main ingredient of success is a good, mutually respectful parent–child relationship. Too many parents ruin that relationship by becoming frustrated and overinvolved in school issues. Love and Logic parents know that a high self-image is the single most important ingredient of success and that the single most important part of a high self-image is a loving relationship with the parents:

• Imposing consequences for poor school performance is necessary at times. But it is dangerous. If the child has a hidden learning problem, it will increase both the parents' and the child's frustration.
• If a child is rebellious, poorly-thought-out consequences increase sneakiness and rebellion. If consequences are to be imposed, don't remove activities that raise the child's self-image, particularly the successful extracurricular activities.

Thurman, who developed the intelligence test, noted near the end of his life that self-image was probably much more important than intelligence per se in predicting success.

© 1998 Foster W. Cline, M.D.

VOLUME

14

Never Let Them See You Sweat

By Jim Fay

VOL. 14, No. 1

I watched a youngster giving his mother fits in the local discount department store. There seemed to be no end to his whining and begging and it was obvious that Mom was on the verge of losing her composure. She continually asked him to settle down, but each request was met with more acting out.

When Mom noticed that the boy's behavior was drawing the attention of other shoppers, she lost what control she had and screamed, "That does it! I've had it with you! Now I'm not buying you anything, so just shut up!"

The child didn't back off that easily. He responded with, "That sucks!"

"Young man, don't you say that word. That's a nasty word. I know your brother says that, but you're not going to do it. I don't want to hear that word out of your mouth again as long as you live. Now you show a little respect!" In a feeble attempt to emphasize her power, she added, "And I mean it!"

Sensing that his mom was now at the end of her rope and had no skills left, he looked right into his mother's eyes and yelled, "Suck, suck, suck, suck, suck! I hate you and you're not going to tell me what to do! I didn't ask to be born into this crummy family!"

Mom's rage got the better of her at this time and she reached out to give him a good slap, which missed completely as he ran down the aisle.

As I watched this episode, I was filled with sadness for both the child and his mother. They are headed for a lot of tough times. Child psychology tells us this child is probably developing subconscious beliefs including:

I'm bad.
My mom is mean.
My mom is powerless.
My mom can try anything she wants, but she can't handle me.

We can all predict what life will be like for these two in future years. Every time Mom tries to control him in this manner, he will think, "My mom can try anything she wants, but she can't handle me." We can fairly accurately predict many arguments, lots of anger, and family chaos.

There is actually a happy ending to this story, proving it's never too late to change the quality of life with our kids.

I managed to get next to this mother in the checkout line, striking up a conversation with, "Isn't it tough raising kids these days? How would you like some laughs to make your days a little better?"

I handed her my card with a note on the back to send it to the Love and Logic Institute for a free copy of one of my audiotapes. I told her there were no strings attached. All she had to do was listen and laugh and then share the tape with her friends. I ended by saying, "Send me a letter and let me know if you enjoyed the tape."

I received a wonderful letter a few months later telling me all about the success she and her friends were having with their kids. And here's the rest of the story.

After listening to her Love and Logic tape, Mom got excited about being able to get back in control with her youngster, Roger. She passed the tape around to some of her friends and before long they all had a common interest in becoming more effective parents. Soon they had formed a support team.

They had a pact that whenever one of them wasn't sure what to do about the behavior of her kids, they would visit on the phone, planning how they would act just like the parents in the stories they were hearing on tape.

Mom created a plan for dealing with Roger and his acting out at the store, which she outlined for her friends. One reacted by saying, "That's great, but what are you going to do if he throws himself on the floor and won't leave with you?"

They thought it over and decided that one of the friends would follow Mom to the store and be available to help. If Roger refused to leave with Mom, she was simply going to walk out of the store. If he didn't follow, the friend would watch to make sure he was safe and then rescue him.

It was agreed that Roger would have to pay for the ride home with some of his favorite toys.

Now that Mom had all the loopholes plugged, she set her plan into motion. The very next day they went shopping. True to form, Roger started begging for things he saw on the shelves. In her calm, rehearsed voice, Mom said, "Not a good idea, Roger. I have to shop without listening to that."

Roger turned up his manipulation a notch with, "Well, I really need those toys. I never get anything. All the other kids get stuff when they go to the store!" He then grabbed two toys off the shelf and threw them into her shopping basket.

At this point, Mom got right close to his face, put a sly grin on, and whispered, "That was a really bad decision, Roger. I'm going to have to do something about that, but not here in the store. I don't want to embarrass you in public. I'll tell you all about it when we get home. Try not to worry about it now." And she gave him a big kiss as she returned the toys to the shelf.

As you can imagine, Mom's new behavior was quite a shock for Roger. This was something he wasn't prepared for. Roger became very quiet at this point and for the rest of their ride home.

As Mom told this story in her letter, she talked of one of the concepts she and her group learned in the Love and Logic studies: *Warning kids of a consequence reduces the power of the consequence.*

This idea helped her keep her cool while she implemented the rest of the plan. She phoned Mable, the baby-sitter from hell, and arranged for her to come over at 10:00 the next morning. She did not tell Roger what was going to happen.

At 10:00 a.m., Mable came to the door. It was at this time that Mom said, "Roger, I'm going to finish my shopping. It's going to be a great day at Target. Do you know why? You won't be there, and I won't have to listen to a five-year-old begging and throwing a fit.

"This will be your first time to hire your own baby-sitter. This is so sad. I know you don't have any money, so you will need to bargain with Mable to see which toys she will accept instead of money. See you later, Sweetie. You have a good time with Mable."

This was a great surprise to Roger, but not to Mable. Mable and Mom had a little side arrangement for payment. Mable had been instructed, also, not to accept any old toys that Roger was tired of. She was only to accept something that would have lasting meaning to the five-year-old. The two adults also had agreed that Mable was not to provide a good time for Roger.

Mom had a wonderful time shopping, making sure that upon her return she was eating an ice cream bar as she walked in the door.

"Hi, Roger. Come give me a hug and let me tell you all about shopping. I had so much fun. I hope you worked out payment with Mable. Shall we send her home so we can have some time together?"

"I don't want her around anymore! Send her home! She made me pay with my Galactic Space Rover and it's new! And she's not fair!"

"I know, Roger. That is so sad. Maybe you need to find a baby-sitter who doesn't charge so much. Well, give me a hug and let's get on with life."

This triumphant mom went on to write that she originally had a concern about the amount of time and planning that went into Roger's training session in the store.

"I didn't think I had it in me to do this with every one of his bad behaviors," she wrote. "However, I got a great surprise. A few days later Roger started throwing a fit about not getting a Happy Meal in the restaurant. I looked at him and sang, "Oh, oh, Roger. Do you think that might be a bad decision?"

Roger's eyes got very wide. He became unusually quiet and stopped complaining.

"I now see why you teach us to learn how to handle one problem in a calm way. There is a great transfer effect. Once Roger saw me handle him without taking a deep breath, he thinks I can do it all the time. And the truth is, I think I can! My life and Roger's are both much better now, thanks to Love and Logic."

© 1998 Jim Fay

CLINE'S CORNER

Love and Logic in the Early Years
By Foster W. Cline, M.D.

VOL. 14, No. 1

Parents often ask how soon they can start using Love and Logic principles. Since Love and Logic is built on a foundation of consequences, Love and Logic starts as soon as the child can understand them.

This generally happens when a child starts throwing the bottle off the high chair for Mom to pick up. Generally, the sequence goes something like this:

1. The child accidentally drops something from the high chair.
2. Mom picks it up.
3. The child accidentally drops something again; with a sigh, Mom picks it up.
4. The child knocks something off on purpose and Mom says, "Keep it on your tray, Susan," picks it up, and gives it back.
5. The child throws the object off the tray and Mom says, "Susan, *stop it!*"

Now the Rant, Rave, and Rescue routines start. And kids love that. Any child would like to play his parents like an electric train: "Now I'm gonna run 'em around the track. Now I'm gonna make 'em jump the track ... Now I'll blow their horn." What fun!

When an infant is old enough to know a behavior bugs his mom, and purposely does it, it's time to start Love and Logic. In this case, Mom should keep her mouth *closed* when she picks up the bottle. She should be noisy with happiness when the child is eating, keeps something from falling, reaches out for more, etc.

Parents who are noisiest when things go wrong have endless difficulty. If the bottle is purposely thrown a second time, Mom smiles, gives the baby a kiss, says "All done," and takes the baby out of the high chair. The meal is over.

During the first four months of life, the rule on how to handle a baby is simple. Do anything you can to keep the baby happy. Snuggle, hold the baby close, have lots of eye contact, touch.

But if the parent keeps this same rule through the first twelve months of life—"I'll do anything I can to keep the baby happy"— you can bet that this mother will be run ragged by a demanding and obnoxious toddler.

The only way a toddler learns to treat other people as if they are important, and subsequently treat himself as important, is through the early interaction in which a mom, by her behavior, says, "Kiddo, I love you and I'm important, too."

One common mistake that often starts early is telling a child what to do but not expecting her to really do it. I've seen a lot of moms who tell their children what to do *before the children understand English!* By the time the children do understand English, they already have learned that what comes out of their mother's mouth has nothing to do with expectations of behavior.

Let's look at two mothers talking to their children as they eat in the high chair at eight months:

CYNTHIA: "Sandy, open up! Wider. Now eat all this. No, don't spit it out. I said no, don't spit. You need to eat your peas. They're good for you. Now don't turn your head. Open up ..."

TRACY: "Sandy ... oh, you keep your mouth closed, don't you? Wow, you turned your head so fast, I almost fed your cheek! Are you saying 'no'? I bet you are. You hate those peas, don't you? I bet you do. Well, maybe we'll try them another day. I think you might like some applesauce. Yes, you do, you little pumpkin ..."

Notice that Cynthia's talk was mainly orders that could never be followed by an eight-month-old. By the time her child understands English, she already knows the commands are meaningless! On the other hand, Tracy chatters to her baby, but doesn't tell her what she has to do.

I remember once, I kiddingly asked a young mom why she didn't just tell her child to eat nicely. She took my silly question seriously, and gave the correct response. "Oh, Foster, I can't tell this baby what to do, because if I ever tell my child what to do, he'll have to do it! And this baby is too young to learn that yet."

I thought to myself, "This young mom has actually *got it!* Good for her!"

The Love and Logic tenet of allowing consequences to fall on the child comes into its own after the child is walking. At that point, kids can get themselves into all sorts of trouble.

Love and Logic parents protect their children so serious harm will not occur. On the other hand, whenever possible they allow their children to *suffer* the consequences of poor decisions.

When a thirteen- or fourteen-month-old toddler begins climbing stairs and has a rough time balancing on padded stair steps, he may have trouble mastering his new skills and locomotion. Moms can handle it in all sorts of ways:

- Ignore the child.
- Request: "Don't climb up and down those stairs, Troy, you'll fall."
- Demand: "Stop it, Troy!"
- Command: "Come over here, Troy, and stand by me."
- Whine: "Troy, please don't."
- Become frustrated and make it even more fun for the child: "I asked you to stop, now I'm not going to ask again. You stop it right now!"

A Love and Logic parent, on the other hand, *thinks* before saying anything (and after a while, one doesn't even have to think, it comes naturally): "Is he likely to hurt himself badly if he falls?"

If yes, "Will he stop if I tell him to?" If yes, ask him to please come off the steps. If no, go *without talking* and pick him up.

If no (he won't hurt himself badly), "Will he learn from this
experience?" Not Troy! (He may be a special needs child.)
Ask him to stop if he would, pick him up if not.

But if he'll probably learn to be more careful, the Love and Logic parent
says, "Troy, Honey, if you continue, there could be a big boom-boom.
There could be an ouchee" (or something to this effect).

We actually hope Troy falls, is not hurt badly, and thinks,
"Mom said this might happen. I'd better listen to my mom next
time, because she's *right!*"

When Troy falls, his mother doesn't say, "Didn't I warn you
about that?!" but hugs him and commiserates, "Oh that's too bad,
Honey. I bet you learned something today."

Generally, toddlers learn their mothers are in control around
two items:

1. "Don't touch."
2. "You need to go sit in your room" (or "on that chair"—said
   while pointing) "until you can decide to act differently" (or
   "until the timer goes bing" or "until I tell you to get up").

On these two things—don't touch and don't move—the toddler
must learn, during the second year of life, that his mother means
business. He *must* respond to those requests. And a few times, with
some children, the mom has to show that she *does* have the power.

These days, it almost seems un-American or certainly politi-
cally incorrect for a parent to show a child that the parent *really*
does have the power. But this is essential during the second year of
life, and can always be carried out in a way that engenders respect
and obedience rather than fear and servitude.

In summary, for a toddler to be happy, she must have a happy
mom who takes loving care of herself by meaning what she says,
and saying what she means. That way, the child develops respect
for her mother and eventually internalizes that into self-respect.

© 1998 Foster W. Cline, M.D.

Loving and Strict at the Same Time
By Jim Fay
VOL. 14, No. 2

I approached one of the Love and Logic schools in our area the other day and met two youngsters standing out front.

"Hi, guys. What are you doing out here during class time?" I asked. I recognized that they were a brother and sister from a somewhat infamous local family with gang ties.

"We got kicked out of school. We're waiting for our parents. We're out of here for three days and we're supposed to do some kind of community service while we're gone!"

"Yeah, man. This is the strictest school we've been at. We've gone to eight different schools already and none of them was as strict as this one!"

"What a bummer," I said. "I bet you hate that."

"No, man. We like this school the best. We never used to care about gettin' kicked out of school, but we like bein' here. We don't want to go home for three days. We'd rather be here."

This was a new one for me, so I had to ask, "How is it that you like this school best when it's the strictest school you've ever attended?"

"Man, they don't put up with our stuff here, but they're real nice about it. They like us even when we've been bad, and they're always helping us to start over again without laying a bunch of extra bad stuff on us when we try to be better."

I couldn't wait to talk with the principal to find out what the staff had been doing that could cause these tough kids to say, "This is the strictest school we've ever been in, and we like it here best of all."

This wise principal told me that running a school well was like doing a great job of parenting. She said it's important to keep it simple, learn a few very effective ways of working with kids, and focus on mastering those techniques. She told me it is better to do a few things really well than to use a lot of different approaches without mastering any of them.

The principal gave the example of a winning football team that knows execution is the secret. Execute a small number of plays perfectly and you're a winner. Throw a great variety of poorly executed plays at the opposing team and it ends up the winner.

"At our school, we have been putting much of our effort this year into perfecting two Love and Logic strategies," the principal offered proudly. "The first thing we have been working on is using delayed consequences.

"The teachers are great at saying, 'That was a bad decision. I'm going to have to do something about that, but not now. I want to get some ideas from the other teachers so I will do something that is really fair. Try not to worry about it until I can get back to you.'"

Her face lit up. She told me morale had improved since staff members began depending on each other to make decisions about working with kids. This happy principal went on to say that the staff's second mission was to perfect its ability to prove to misbehaving kids that the adults care about them and are empathetic and understanding.

"Empathy must be locked in before describing the consequence the misbehaving child will receive," she said. "Our teachers frequently remind each other to 'lock in your empathy before you lower the boom.'"

"Let me give you an example," she said. "I used to feel I had to be angry whenever I had to suspend a kid for fighting. I guess I thought it would help convince the kid that he had been bad and needed to shape up. My old approach went like this:

'Why are you always fighting? You know that fighting is against the rules! You knew that before you got into the fight! You knew the punishment for fighting is a three-day suspension. You're out of here until Friday, and the next time I see you in this office it had better be for something good! Now call your mom and have her pick you up.'

"Compare this to my new way," she beamed. "Now I lock in my empathy before I lower the boom:

'Oh, no, another fight. What a bummer. You must really be having a hard time with the other kids. I sure hope you find a better way. But I can understand a kid wanting to fight. By the way, what is the punishment for fighting around here?'

'Three days?'

'You got it, pal. When will we get to see you again?'

'Friday, I guess.'

'Well, this is really a bummer for you. We'll look forward to seeing you on Friday. Do you need to call someone to pick you up? See ya, pal.'"

Before this excited principal perfected this technique she was always the "bad guy" in the eyes of the students. "Now," she reflected, "I'm usually the good guy and their bad decisions play the bad-guy role. I go home a lot more refreshed at the end of each day."

Locking in Empathy on the Home Front

It is very difficult for most parents to lock in their empathy before consequencing children. Even when we know the right thing to do, our childhood conditioning takes over when kids do something wrong.

Parents who are most successful at locking in their empathy before lowering the boom don't try to think up loving, empathetic, or understanding statements in the face of a problem.

Instead, they memorize one or two statements they can recall at the drop of a hat. They use the same statements each time and they say them with sincerity. Some examples:

"What a bummer."

"How sad."

"Oh, no. That's never good."

✓ Step One: Pick one of these statements or make up a favorite of your own. Write it over and over on scraps of paper, and stick it on your dashboard, in your mind, or on the inside of your eyelids. (Have I made a point?) Keep this phrase on the tip of your tongue at all times.

✓ Step Two: Fall asleep at night visualizing yourself using this phrase when your child does something wrong.

✓ Step Three: Pray for your child to make a mistake so you can practice your new skill.

✓ Step Four: Remember that it's best to delay consequencing a child until you are calm, have a clear head, and have secured the advice of friends.

✓ Step Five: Enjoy the power you have over yourself and the change in your child's attitude.

Consider the following example in which an angry teen has slammed the bedroom door so hard that a picture has fallen off the wall, breaking the glass and the frame:

PARENT: "Oh, no, Turner. What a bummer."

TURNER: "It's your fault. You made me so mad!"

PARENT: "What a bummer. I guess I'm going to have to do something about this, but not right now. I'll get back to you. I need to get some ideas first. Try not to worry about it."

TURNER: "You're the one who needs to worry, 'cause it's your fault."

PARENT: "I love you too much to argue with you about that. We'll talk later."

This parent then spends some time clearing her head and practicing the delivery of the consequence, before giving it:

PARENT: "What happened to the picture frame was a real bummer. I can understand your getting mad and slamming the door. I also don't think you meant to destroy anything. Here's the phone number of a business that can help you fix it. Thanks."

TURNER: "Well, I still don't think I should have to pay for that."

PARENT: "I understand. I usually feel the same way. Thanks for getting it fixed."

Working with a child is always easier when both adult and child are calm, and when the adult is genuinely sympathetic. These Love and Logic ideas are designed to help you enjoy raising your kids. I hope they do the job for you.

Toothbrush Lies
By Charles Fay, Ph.D.
VOL. 14, NO. 2

How many battles do you suppose take place between parents and their kids over toothbrushing?

After one of my Love and Logic presentations, a couple came to me and described all the troubles they used to have getting their four-year-old-son, Stevie, to brush. Each morning, one of them would turn to Stevie and say, "Okay, we need to hurry. Please go brush your teeth."

Stevie would run into his bedroom and hide under the bed. Suddenly Dad would notice that Stevie was missing. He'd search the house and finally find Stevie hiding under his bed. About to blow a gasket, Dad would grumble, "Did you brush your teeth yet?"

"I don't *want* to!" Stevie would complain. Frustrated beyond belief, Dad would grab Stevie by the arm and yell, "How many times do I have to ask you to brush your teeth?! You get in that bathroom and brush your teeth!"

A small smile would creep onto Stevie's face. "You think this is funny?!" Dad would yell. "You think this is a big joke?! If I'm late for work again, we aren't going to McDonald's this weekend! You can forget about watching a movie tonight!"

Pulling himself free and collapsing to the floor, Stevie would begin to scream and cry, "I want to go to McDonald's! I want to go! I want to go!"

Desperate, Dad would take Stevie's arm and try to drag him to the sink. Have you ever noticed how well little kids can resist by making their bodies completely limp? Having no success, Dad would eventually give up and carry Stevie into the bathroom. On the way, he'd give the age-old "Your Teeth Are Gonna Fall Out" lecture. Nevertheless, Stevie still resembled a limp rag!

At the sink, Dad would put Stevie's small feet on a little step-stool and say, "Okay, let's get this done—I'm already late!"

Stevie would shake his head. "No!"

After five or ten minutes of struggle, one of Stevie's front teeth would have a small dab of toothpaste on it and he'd be blowing white bubbles with the toothpaste and looking like a rabid dog.

At their wit's end, Mom and Dad would carry him to the car, deposit him at the daycare center, and race to work. Both of them were late—again!

What a frustrating ordeal for these parents! Was Stevie leading them around the house with an invisible leash?

Love and Logic parents learn to regain control of their homes by following two simple rules:

✓ 1. Parents take good care of themselves by providing limits in a loving way.
✓ 2. Parents replace punishment with equal parts of empathy and logical consequences.

After the couple finished telling this part of their story, the mother began to smile and said, "But we've been studying Love and Logic and a lot of this stuff has been making sense and working." Then she frowned and added, "But we had a big problem with your *Toddlers and Preschoolers* audio."

Before I asked her what the problem was, the smile returned to her face, and she told me their success story.

It was a typical Monday morning, with both of them trying to get ready for work. Stevie sat on the living room floor playing with some toys. Mom kneeled next to him and asked him softly, "Have you brushed your teeth, Sweetheart?"

Stevie looked up, paused, and then began to nod. "I did it, Mommy. Yes."

Suspicious, Mom walked upstairs, went to the sink, and felt his little toothbrush. Dry as a bone!

About this time, do you imagine she was forgetting all about Love and Logic and thinking she ought to just wring his little neck instead? He'd thrown her a curve! He'd never lied about brushing before, and she was temporarily thrown off balance. Then she remembered one comforting thought she'd learned from Love and Logic: "Anger and frustration feed misbehavior."

And she kept repeating this to herself as she grappled for how to handle the situation. "Anger and frustration feed misbehavior ... Anger and frustration feed misbehavior."

Then she suddenly remembered a second thing she had learned from Love and Logic: "It's okay to delay a consequence until I'm calm and have a plan." And she kept repeating this to herself as she walked down the stairs.

Stevie was still playing with his toys. Mom walked over to him, kneeled down, and said, "This is really sad. I need to know you will tell me the truth about things."

Stevie sat still, silently studying the carpet.

Mom continued, "You didn't brush your teeth."

Stevie continued to stare at the floor, studying the carpet fibers.

Mom stood and walked away. "It's just sad," she said. "I'll have to do something about this, but not right now. Try not to worry about what's going to happen."

Stevie looked up with eyes wide. "What are you going to do?"

Mom gave a sad smile. "Try not to worry."

Stevie continued, "Tell me! Am I in trouble?"

As Mom walked into the other room she said sadly, "Probably so."

As the morning unfolded, Mom and Dad got ready for work, ate breakfast, and dropped Stevie at daycare. They met for lunch to put together a plan.

That evening, Stevie gobbled down his macaroni and cheese, jumped down from the dinner table, ran to the kitchen counter, and said, "I made a happy plate, Mommy. I finished! I want my blue sucker—the one with gum inside."

Mom and Dad were really tempted now! Tempted to say something like, "Forget it!"

Instead, Dad put on a sad face, turned to Stevie, and said, "Mommy and I give treats to kids who protect their teeth by brushing."

Stevie turned from the counter. "I brushed 'em—I did it!"

Mom responded, "This is so sad. We give treats to kids who brush."

Stevie Screamed, "I did it! I want my sucker! *I hate you!*"

Dad responded with empathy, "We will love you."

Stevie continued with this lollipop mantra: "I want it, I want it, I want it."

Mom asked, "Can you be nice and stay with us?"

The mantra continued and intensified: "I want it! I want it! *I want it!*"

Then Dad looked sad for Stevie and sang, "Uh ohhh, looks like a little bedroom time. This is so sad." As he talked, he walked over to Stevie, gently scooped him up into his arms, and silently carried him to his room.

Stevie wasn't so silent. "No! I hate you, Daddy! No! No! No!"

Walking out of Stevie's room, Dad asked, "Can you be quiet and stay in your room, or do you need me to lock your door?"

Stevie screamed and threw his teddy bear.

Dad ducked, closed the door, latched it, and sat on the floor just outside as Stevie had the fit of all fits, throwing his toys against the door, yelling, screaming, and crying.

After close to forty-five minutes of full-fledged four-year-old fury, the room became quiet. Dad slowly opened the door to see Stevie all sweaty and weeping softly on his bed. He walked over to Stevie's bed, sat down, hugged his little son, and said, "Let's go read a book before bed."

Mom, Dad, and little Stevie sat on the couch reading a bedtime story. As Mom finished the book, Stevie yawned and rubbed his eyes. "Sweetheart, let's go upstairs and get ready for bed," said Mom. As Stevie walked up the stairs holding Mom's hand, she asked, "Will you go brush your teeth, Stevie?"

Stevie dropped to the floor. "I don't want to, Mommy," he whined.

Mom looked down at him with a warm grin and asked, "Who do Mommy and Daddy give treats to?"

Dad turned to him, grinned, raised his eyebrows, and said, "Uh ohhhhhh."

Stevie's eyebrows lifted a bit too, as he ran into the bathroom, squeezed a dab of toothpaste onto his little toothbrush, and went to work on his teeth.

Mom and Dad sat on the bed next to him and said, "Goodnight, Sweetie. We love you."

Stevie started to cry. Then he looked up and said, "Mommy? Daddy? Do you love me even when I'm bad?"

"Oh, yes!" they said. "Sometimes we just don't like the way you behave."

Stevie continued, "You know that music tape with the man talking on it about boys?"

Mom and Dad looked at each other, then at Stevie, and asked, "What music tape?"

Stevie, still crying, said, "That one with the baby and he put his food on the dog?"

Dad suddenly realized what Stevie was talking about. "The *Toddlers* tape! What about it?" he asked.

Stevie mumbled, "I took it out of Mommy's car."

Mom jumped in, "Where is it?"

After a long pause filled with tears and sniffling, Stevie cried, "I put it down the potty 'cause I don't like that man saying, 'uh ohh-hhhh' like Daddy does."

Stevie's parents suddenly understood why the toilet had been overflowing that evening, and I suddenly understood the "big problem" they'd had with their *Toddlers* tape.

How they handled this problem was a whole different story— a story about how little Stevie learned to pay for a new *Toddlers* tape, and for a visit from the plumber, with toys and chores around the house.

Stevie's parents followed just two rules to motivate him to brush his teeth. First, they set limits by telling Stevie what *they* would do, rather than trying to boss him around. "Mommy and Daddy give treats to kids who brush" is clearly easier to enforce and more effective than "You get in that bathroom and brush—now!"

Stevie's parents also learned how to "lock in" the empathy before delivering consequences. "This is so sad" forced Stevie to own the pain of his misbehavior rather than blaming it on his parents. From this empathy, the "Uh, Oh Song," and paying for the damage he had caused, he learned four essential things.

First, when Mom and Dad say something, I better listen. Second, Mom and Dad won't be manipulated by temper tantrums and arguing. Third, when I make a problem for others, I'll end up having to fix it—and that will be so sad for me. Fourth, Mom and Dad love me enough to set limits, follow through, and expect me to be the very best kid I can be.

Wouldn't we all love to give our kids these gifts?

© 1998 Charles Fay, Ph.D.

CLINE'S CORNER

Fast Food Fiascoes
By Foster W. Cline, M.D.
VOL. 14, NO. 2

What's cheap, quick, and has a playground? A fast food restaurant! I love watching families interact in fast food restaurants. I see moms and dads lovingly enjoying time with their kids. Some families make me think, "What a sweet mom and dad they are!" They take me back to loving times at the Golden Arches when my own children were small.

But there are other families who make me think a whole slew of other thoughts:

"When those kids are teenagers, Mom, you will deserve them!"

"Those kids have the parents well trained."

"Mom, you think it's cute now, but it'll be pure pain when he's fifteen!"

"Oh my gosh, they think he's precocious—but he's obnoxious!"

"If she won't even help clean up the french fries, good luck having her help with the dishes!"

Queen of the Food Queue

Standing in line behind the Queen of the Food Queue is not really enjoyable. It is two-thirds annoying and one-third interesting. The Queen is usually four to six years old and stands in line with her parents, none thinking about what they will have for lunch until they are finally at the counter and are asked, "What would you like?"

This initiates a flurry of mental gymnastics as Mom and Dad decide what they want and then ask the Queen, "What would you like, Honey?" Big mistake. The Queen first asks for things the joint doesn't have. Mom replies, "They don't have Kiddy Joy Meals here, so what else would you like?"

After a great deal of hemming and hawing—all of this occurs when the line is fairly long, and folks are really hungry—the parents begin to make suggestions. But the Queen will have none of these suggestions. She asks if she can have an ice cream cone, and is told she has to eat lunch first, and then maybe the family will stop by Baskin-Robbins.

This subtle attempt to bribe the child into making a decision leads her to ratchet up her requests to plaintive wails for a plastic toy like she got last week when she ordered her Kiddy Joy Meal. It is explained that they have a nice Disney cup for her here instead.

This only marginally mollifies the Queen, who eventually decides what she wants, and the whole family finally shuffles off to the table for Mom and Dad to wait on her there.

I remember the old days when my Love and Logic wife, while we stood in line, asked the children if they would like a hamburger, or chicken bits, or nothing. If they knew what they wanted before she got to the counter, it was their choice. If they didn't know before being asked, it was Mom's choice.

The French Fry Fracas

Some little boys just can't wait till they're on the ball field to take their turn at pitching. And I hear moms—less often the dads—say, "Now turn around and quit throwing french fries" as the kid continues to toss them across the table at his sister.

I think of all the things parents could say when their kid throws french fries. There are dozens of statements that would work:

> "Guthro, there are several ways to enjoy your fries. If you enjoy them by eating them and not throwing them, I know they won't be the last ones you see for a month."
>
> "Hey, Tabor, you have the choice of eating your french fries here or saving them to throw in the garbage at home and cleaning them up if you miss the can."
>
> "Sweetheart, will you please give me your french fries so I can save them for the dog? Thank you."
>
> "Wade, I would appreciate your not throwing french fries. I'm sure you would be real unhappy if it continued. Why would you be unhappy? I'd tell you, but I don't think you'd want to be that unhappy yet."

The point is, there are literally dozens of effective things to say to a child who throws french fries. The only thing a parent shouldn't do is say, "Don't throw french fries" and then allow the kid to toss another tuber.

Parents can't ask the kids to help clean up, and then do all the cleaning up themselves. Wise parents give choices and say what they mean, mean what they say, and say it once!

Good Times in Playland

Fast food restaurants have installed entire playpens filled with big plastic tubes and little plastic balls as each chain tries to prove itself the most kid-friendly. What could be a better deal for the parents than a place where kids are actually encouraged to leave their parents in peace to nibble the leftover french fries?

112

Alas, the playpens also provide the kids with a new proving ground for parent training:

> "Now where did you put your shoes? We've got to go."
> "Cathy, please play nice!"
> "Troy, please stop hurting that little boy you keep flattening at the bottom of the slide."

Happy demands of "Hey, look at me" drift from the second story of the pen while adults below interrupt their conversations to look up and comment approvingly.

But every so often, a Love and Logic mom walks in. She immediately distinguishes herself from the rabble by the loving smiles she exchanges with her generally well-behaved children. And she is always talking choices: "Honey, have fun in Playland after you finish eating. If you have trouble handling it, or you lose your shoes, don't worry. We don't have to come here next time."

Recently I was asked, "Foster, in a fast food restaurant I noticed one mom with a three- or four-year-old boy who had to eat before he could play, but by the time we left after fifteen minutes he hadn't taken a bite. Another little girl, about two, was valiantly trying not to cry, and losing the battle, after being allowed to play for five minutes and then having to leave."

It's so easy to have fun with fast food when children are given choices:

> "When you finish and clean up your lunch, please feel free to go to the play area. You don't need to go to the play area today."
> "Honey, if you play in the play area today for five minutes and then leave happily, you'll be able to play here every time we come. Of course, I want this time at 'Fast Food' to be fun for both us both."

There's nothing like a fast food place to make clear the difference between the parent who uses choices, consequences, and concern and the one who uses demands and rants and raves.

A Lesson Well Learned
By Jim Fay
VOL. 14, NO. 3

My mailbox has been rich with stories from parents who provide great tips for raising kids. Each one is a new application of the two rules of Love and Logic:

Rule One: Take care of yourself in a healthy, loving way.
Rule Two: When a kid causes a problem, hand the problem
back in a loving way.

A Texas mom gives us a great example of this with a story about her seventeen-year-old, who is working this summer. The new job doesn't give the mom and son much time together, so she offered to take him out to eat dinner at one of his favorite restaurants once a week.

This mother is one who expects her boy to treat her with respect, thereby learning the manners and courtesies that should help carry him far in his life. When they go out in public, he is expected to be polite, assist her with her chair in the restaurant, hold the door for his mother, etc.

On this special night out they decided not to drive all the way into the big city, but to eat at a favorite restaurant only three miles from home.

All went well on their "date" until they arrived. The youngster got out of the car and headed straight for the front door of the restaurant instead of opening the car door for his mother. Somewhat exasperated, she got out of the car tried to keep up with him as he trudged into the restaurant.

Her thoughts were, "Maybe he has a lot on his mind. He's worked hard all day. He's probably tired. I guess I can be understanding this one time."

But wait! Things got worse. He didn't hold the door to the restaurant open for her. Instead, he barged through the door, letting it swing back and smack her right in the face. He didn't even look back, apologize, or make an attempt to help his mother. He just went about his business as though she wasn't there.

What a shock! Mom was no longer the understanding, loving mother of a seventeen-year-old. She was fired up. Standing outside the restaurant, fighting the urge to kill, she got in touch with her Love and Logic training. Fortunately, there are only two rules for her to remember: Take care of herself and hand the problem back to the kid.

She said to herself, "If I allow this, I'm not taking good care of myself. If I allow this, I'm letting him hand me the problem. I'm not going to be the victim here."

With defiance flashing in her eyes, she turned around, got into the car, and drove home. All this time she was thinking, "Let him worry about me for a change. Let him figure out how to get his dinner. Let him figure out how to get home. I bet if his girlfriend was three miles away, he could figure out how to get transportation to see her. He'll get home just fine on his own."

Later that evening he arrived at home. By that time he was quite concerned about what had happened to his mother.

"Where were you? What happened? I looked all over the restaurant. I even had some lady go into the restroom to see if you were okay. But you weren't anywhere. I looked in the parking lot and the car was gone. I had to borrow money from the manager of the restaurant to eat dinner 'cause I was really hungry. And then I had to walk all the way home. It was three miles. What happened?"

Mom had been spending a lot of time thinking about how to handle this problem. The length of the evening gave her plenty of time to get herself under control and practice how she was going to talk with her son. She had been thinking that even though he's usually a pretty sensitive kid, it wasn't good for him to get away with such poor manners.

Reflecting back on her use of the Love and Logic rules, she asked herself, "Did I take care of myself? Yes, I came home and fixed myself a nice meal. Did I hand the problem back? I sure did. He had a lot of problems as a result of my actions. Good for me!"

Her answer to the youngster's concern about what happened was a very controlled, "As soon as that door slammed in my face, I told myself that only a fool would buy a meal for someone with those kinds of manners. So I went home and had a nice meal all by myself. I'm glad, though, that you figured out how to get your own dinner and I'm especially glad that you found a way to get home."

"Wow, Mom, I was really worried about you. I thought something terrible had happened. I'm glad you're okay. Three miles is a really long way to walk after you've been working all day. It's a good thing we decided not to go all the way into the city for dinner tonight. I would have really been in trouble!"

This mom demonstrates an artistic application of the Love and Logic principles. She understands that parents don't take good care of themselves when they throw adult temper tantrums over childhood misbehavior. They are not taking care of themselves when they excuse any bad behaviors. They are not taking care of themselves when they use anger, lectures, threats, and warnings.

She understands that if she had done any of these things, she would have created a situation in which the youngster would have become emotional, defensive, argumentative, or belligerent. The kid's focus of attention would have been on what a bad person the adult was instead of what a bad decision the youngster made.

This mom's approach kept the problem on the child's shoulders. This seventeen-year-old spent most of his energy worrying about Mom, solving the problem, and thinking about how lucky he was not having to walk a lot farther. And as a bonus, his relationship with his mom is still good. Let's give this great mom a tip of the hat.

© 1998 Jim Fay

Why Siblings Fight—And What to Do About It
By Charles Fay, Ph.D.

VOL. 14, NO. 3

How many times do parents hear one of their kids screaming something like this: "Daaad! Brian won't stop picking on me! Make him stop!"

And then Brian whines, "No I didn't! Lisa started it! Why do I always get blamed for everything around here?"

Does this sound familiar? Do you ever feel as though your kids act more like hungry alley cats fighting over the last mouse in town than the loving sibs you'd hoped they'd grow to be? You are not alone!

What's a parent to do when the kids are at each other's throats and the living room looks like finals at the international wrestling championship? The first step toward success is understanding some of the reasons why siblings bicker and fight. Why is it that our children—our flesh and blood—often go for flesh and blood?

Let's first recognize that sibling conflicts are generally a pretty typical and normal part of family life. In fact, one might argue that these conflicts are good training for life. That is, by negotiating childhood conflicts with their brothers or sisters, our kids learn valuable skills for getting along with others in the real world.

For this learning to happen, the following must take place in the home:

1. Children must witness their parents working out disagreements in a cooperative and nonviolent manner. Kids learn a lot from watching us.
2. Parents must place primary responsibility for solving sibling conflicts on the parties involved—the kids! In other words, parents stay out of it.
3. Parents share ideas on how the conflict might be resolved in a healthy manner.

Another reason siblings fight is because it gets them attention and control. When parents yell or lecture to determine "who started it," to get their kids to "knock it off," or to get their children to "say sorry and shake hands," the parents are doing more thinking and worrying than the kids!

Soon the children learn on an unconscious level that they can control the color of their parents' faces, the volume of their voices, their reserves of emotional energy, and the potential longevity of their cardiovascular systems.

And have you ever noticed how your kids tend to start a fight just as you start talking on the phone or start a quiet conversation with your spouse? What better way to control your parents?

Fortunately, parents can do three things to keep their children from learning these unhealthy patterns:

1. Parents take care of themselves by making sure the conflict happens somewhere they can't see or hear it. They say, "Feel free to continue this argument someplace where it doesn't hassle my eyes or ears."
2. If the parents are interrupted or inconvenienced by the fighting, they say, "This is so sad. How are you going to repay us for interrupting our conversation? Raking the yard will do."
3. If one or both children resist completing the chore, the parent calmly says, "I'll be happy to do the things I do for you around here when you decide to contribute to this family by doing chores." The parent "goes on strike" until the child complies. In the meantime, the child can survive on "boring" and "yucky" food like apples, oranges, cold fried chicken, etc.

A third reason siblings fight is because one child in the family feels that the parents or other adults see him or her as being the "black sheep" of the family. He or she reasons on an unconscious level, "I'll never be as good as my brother. Everybody thinks he's so smart ... He's such a goody-two-shoes ... I hate him!"

In most cases, the child doesn't really hate his or her sibling. Instead, he or she hates the feeling of not measuring up in the eyes of the parents. The parents may not view the child in this manner. Nevertheless, the most important point is that the child "feels" it to be so.

Parents and teachers can do two things to help avoid this problem:

1. Don't compare kids with each other. One of the most damaging statements I ever heard was made in the local K-Mart store by a frustrated father: "Why can't you just sit and be good like your brother?"
2. Celebrate your children's differences and focus primary energy on helping them identify and build upon their strengths. Research clearly shows us that personality and learning differences begin at or before birth. The more we try to make our kids the same, the more frustrated and angry everyone in the family becomes.

Help all of your children learn that everyone is different, and that everyone has something positive to contribute.

A fourth reason has to do with much more serious and dangerous types of problems. In rare instances, one or more children in the family—or the entire family—is experiencing such severe emotional distress that the rivalry has become dangerous.

What's a parent to do if he or she sees this happening with children? Here are some suggestions:

1. Don't ignore the problem. Make sure the children are adequately supervised and that they are not allowed to inflict serious damage upon each other. This is the one instance in which parents must intervene to ensure safety.

   Caution! With older children and teens, avoid trying to physically separate them. Call 911 or the police department for assistance if the conflict becomes violent.
2. Don't hesitate to get professional help from a competent psychologist or therapist. There are solutions to these types of

sibling conflicts, but these solutions require family therapy and ongoing work with a solid mental health professional.

Once we've gotten a handle on what might be causing rivalry and conflicts between our children, it's time to take action! Recently, I received a letter from a mom who was using Love and Logic. It read something like this:

Dear Dr. Fay,

I'm writing this letter to tell you about my two sons. Mike is eight and Eric is ten. They used to argue and fight constantly, and my husband and I were about to pull our hair out. Then one night we decided to use some Love and Logic.

This night, near the end of December, our boys wanted to go camping in the front yard. They wanted to set up their tent and pretend. Since it's been in the twenties and thirties at night lately, I told them they could set up their tent in the living room or the basement instead.

Boy, did this ever start a fight! Eric wanted to camp in the basement, but Mike wanted to camp in the living room.

My husband and I decided to stay out of it and let them work it out. They did! Mike gave in to Eric, and they both ran off to the basement to arrange their campsite. About 2:00 in the morning we heard a horrible sound. Eric and Mike ran into our bedroom pushing and shoving.

Eric screamed, "Mom! Daaad! Mike bit me!" Then he held up his arm. No blood, but some slight teeth marks.

Mike started screaming too. "He started it! He started it!"

My husband and I were so frustrated we felt like strangling them. Instead, I remembered to use sadness instead of anger. I also remembered that it is okay to delay a consequence until you have a plan.

I looked at my boys and said, "Oh no, guys. Bad decision waking us up. Guess your father and I will have to do something about this tomorrow. Try not to worry about it."

It was great! I'd never seen them look so confused. Then my husband said, "Go ahead and fight somewhere that won't keep us awake."

When the boys continued to argue, I said, "The longer you keep us awake, the sadder it's going to be for you tomorrow."

The next morning, both of them came to us and asked what we were going to do. My husband told them they could take the day to think about how they might make it up to us by doing some chores.

During dinner that evening, I could tell both of them were about to explode. Finally, they couldn't take it any longer and told us they wanted to wash our cars to make up for the problem.

My husband said, "That's a start. Throw in cleaning the bathtubs and toilets and we have a deal." The funniest thing was that the boys actually looked relieved!

Now, when the boys start fighting, we just look at them and say something like, "This is so sad. I wonder if you'll need to do some chores to pay us back for all this noise and hassle."

It's amazing how quickly they stop arguing. This doesn't always work. But that's good, because then I get a break from some of my chores! Sometimes I even find myself looking forward to their fights.

Sincerely,
A Happier Mom

CLINE'S CORNER

Extracurricular Activities: To Be or Not to Be?

By Foster W. Cline, M.D.

Vol. 14, No. 3

A mother laments: "I never see my eleven-year-old. He is in competitive soccer and a good gymnast. Now he is in band. How much is too much?"

Another mom decided to home-school her children—for one thing, with all the kids' activities, she wanted to see them more! I have talked to a number of moms who feel that "chauffeur" is their main job description.

On the other hand, extracurricular activities are important. Most provide children with opportunities for teamwork, individualized goals, responsibilities, and rewards for practice and perseverance.

Adults look back on their extracurricular activities as among the most meaningful aspects of childhood. Many adults carry on childhood avocations as part of an adult vocation.

I know of those who rode horses in childhood who became horse trainers and vets in adulthood. Those who played in the city park went on to play in the ball park. Adult maestros and virtuosos built on a foundation of childhood music lessons.

In fact, studies have shown that adulthood high achievement correlates more with performance and enjoyment of childhood extracurricular activities than it does with childhood academic performance!

Parents who want high-achieving adults would do just as well to focus on and congratulate their children for their game results as for report-card performance.

It is the universal recognition of the enrichment that extracurricular activities bring to children that makes parental decisions concerning where to draw the line on participation so very difficult.

However, there are answers.

Love and Logic Guidelines on Extracurricular Activities
There are three basic considerations:

1. What does the child want?
2. Objectively, how is the child doing?
3. What is the activity's impact on family operations?

Rule 1: If the child is doing well, and wants it, continue it.
I have counseled many parents who feel their high-achieving child "needs to slow down." I often feel the parents who are concerned about this may need to slow down themselves! Their advocating childhood slowdown is really a projection of their own needs.

In addition, an extracurricular activity that a child excels in generally should not be taken away because of poor academic performance. Other imposed consequences are effective and less detrimental to self-image than eliminating an activity that leads the child to feel good about him- or herself.

Rule 2: If a child doesn't want it, and is performing poorly, stop it! One would think this rule is common sense. But there are lots of kids who hate piano, stare at the keys, and still take lessons because parents insist on it. Or who hate practice, watch the ball roll between their immobile feet, and still are on the team because dad played ball in college.

When enjoyment in the activity is gone, and it is only done because of obligation, then generally stop it. Parents never should set themselves up for resentment by buying expensive instruments or other equipment for extracurricular activities. Rent it until you are sure the child will continue and excel in the activity.

Rule 3: If the child wants it and performs poorly or doesn't practice, make sure the child pays for the activity. When Susan practices flute, her mom pays for lessons. When she forgets to practice once during the week, Susan pays for half the lesson. If she forgets or doesn't practice twice, Susan pays for the entire lesson.

Rule 4: Impact on family operations is primary. A child's extra-curricular activities can fragment family cohesiveness. Many of today's families simply spend no time together. Mom does her activities, the children theirs, and Dad's never home!

First, the parent or parents need to sit down and as adults decide: How much family time per week do we really want together? How important is that time? What are we willing to give up to achieve it?

Many times I have found that these important adult questions simply aren't asked! Obviously, if the questions aren't asked, answers aren't found and the adults go around with a feeling that things should somehow be "different." One can't expect a child to meet unspoken or unrecognized family togetherness requirements.

However, parents of some adolescents use the family "togetherness" issue to force an adolescent who should be out there "doing their thing" to attend a family picnic that is utterly boring and uninteresting—even to many of the adults who attend. Common sense needs to be applied here.

Generally, if a child's activities are detrimental to family operations, cohesiveness, and togetherness, parents and children need to sit down in a problem-solving session to reach a compromise.

© 1998 Foster W. Cline, M.D.

"My Party Will Be Ruined If You and Mom Are in the House"

By Jim Fay

VOL. 14, NO. 4

TEEN: "Dad, there's no way you can be at the party. My social life will be ruined if you're supervising my party. Why can't you just go somewhere else for the evening so I can have a real party? Don't you realize what you're doing to my social life?"

How many parents do you know who have given in to this kind of teenage logic and allowed their kids to have unsupervised parties? Some parents give in because they are desperate for their teens to be popular. Some give in because they are afraid of alienating their kids and have a history of allowing their kids to hold them hostage.

And there are probably many other reasons that parents allow unsupervised parties, leaving their kids and themselves vulnerable to:

1. Potential lawsuits resulting from teen drinking or drug use.
2. Raising wild, irresponsible kids.
3. Having their house destroyed by uninvited guests.
4. Raising kids who are used to getting their way through manipulation.
5. Missed opportunities to share and enforce values and principles.
6. Criminal liability.

The bad news is that saying no to teens is not an easy thing to do. It is especially difficult for parents who did not start out their parenting lives setting and enforcing limits for their kids.

Setting limits is also very difficult for many parents because the only techniques they know are the ones their parents used. Even if those techniques worked for parents in the past, they usually do not work on today's kids.

When my dad told me not to do something, I knew he had the backing of all the other parents in the neighborhood, and the rest of society, as well. Actually, he could be pretty sloppy with his techniques because I knew I couldn't go crying to Child Protection Services or Social Services, or anyone else, to make him change his mind. Dad's word was the last word on the subject.

I also knew that if any of my neighbors saw me misbehaving, a report quickly would go to my father. Everyone on the block had an interest in me behaving.

I remember complaining to one of the neighbors about his telling my dad about something I did, and he quickly said to me,

"You're going to grow up and live in our neighborhood, so you better learn to be a good citizen."

I'm afraid those days may be over. Many neighbors are shy about reporting a child's misdeeds out of fear of being labeled a troublemaker or being told to stay out of other people's business.

The good news is that we no longer need to rely on the old skills that don't work on today's kids. New and powerful skills are available and easy to learn. Before we examine these new skills, let's examine how the old skills—reasoning, ordering, and demanding—work with today's teen:

TEEN: "My party is just going to be ruined if you and Mom supervise. Why can't you just go somewhere else and leave us alone? You're going to ruin my social life!"

DAD: "You don't need an unsupervised party. Your friends will understand."

TEEN: "No they won't. None of the other parents spy on their kids when they have parties."

DAD: "Don't give me that. No responsible parent would allow an unsupervised party."

TEEN: "Oh, sure, when you were kids, but now is now. All the other kids have parties without their parents treating them like babies. I'll be the laughing stock of the whole school."

DAD: "Well, Katy, as long as you live in my house you will do what I say. I don't care what other parents do."

TEEN: "There you go. You're such a control freak. You don't care anything about me. Well, if you loved me, you'd trust me. That's the problem, you don't trust me!"

DAD: "We trust you. It's your friends we worry about."

TEEN: "There you go on my friends! At least they're not like your hypocritical friends, always telling their kids not to drink, and they're always drinking like fish. They drink a lot worse than their kids do."

DAD: "You keep my friends out of this. At least they're old enough to drink legally."

TEEN: "Yeah, but we're not going to be drinking at my party. And I'm going to be sure everyone takes real good care of the house. I don't know why you have to make such a big deal out of a little party. If I can't have one little party without a bunch of adults spying on us, how am I ever going to be able to show my face at school? You don't want everyone to think I'm weird, do you? Please. Why can't you just trust me for once?"

It is obvious that this parent is working very hard to appeal to the teen's sense of reason. However, reasoning never works with kids. Kids play by a different set of rules that don't include reason, accuracy, and common sense. Their rule is: "Win at any cost."

Notice that the parent's attempt to issue an order fell on deaf ears. Many of today's kids view demands as the first step in the negotiation or manipulation process.

Wise words: Never reason with a child. There is nothing about a child that a little reasoning won't make worse.

LOVE AND LOGIC TIP:
1. Lead with empathy or understanding.
2. Follow with a question.
3. End with some choices.

Let's listen as a parent handles the same problem using the Love and Logic approach. Notice that the parent does no reasoning, explaining, or demanding.

Instead, this parent is going to, first of all, demonstrate caring by listening and trying to understand. Next, the parent is going to take some private time to clear his head, seek advice from others, and then identify some choices. This wise father is going to offer some choices that he likes, not one he likes and one he doesn't like:

TEEN: "Dad, there's no way you can be at the party. My social life will be ruined if you're supervising my party. Why can't you just go somewhere else for the evening so I can have a real party? Don't you realize what you're doing to my social life?"

DAD: "Why is this so important to you?"

TEEN: "If you guys are spying on us, how can we have any fun?"

DAD: "Are you going to be doing stuff I don't approve of?"

TEEN: "Of course not, but none of my friends have their parents at their parties. Everybody will think I'm weird. You don't want other kids to think I'm weird, do you? You don't realize what it'll do to my social life."

DAD: "This is pretty important to you, then?"

TEEN: "Yeah, I don't want everybody to see you treating me like a baby. I'm not a baby. I'm sixteen. A lot of girls have babies by then, and I can't even have a party without my parents breathing down my neck. All I want is one little party. It's not like I'm drinking and drugging like a lot of kids. You should appreciate that I'm not like that."

DAD: "I can see you really want to have an unsupervised party. I'm not sure how to react to that. I need some time to think it over and see if there are any choices I can live with. I'll let you know by Friday. Thanks for letting me know how important this is to you."

Dad and Mom talk this over in private and agree there is no way they can allow this unsupervised party. They brainstorm some choices and decide another talk with their daughter is needed:

PARENT: "Katy, we've been thinking about your unsupervised party. And we've also been thinking about our legal responsibilities."

TEEN: "So?"

PARENT: "We've thought of three choices. You can decide."

TEEN: "What?"
PARENT: "The first choice is to have the party with us in the house. We will try to stay out of the way."
TEEN: "No way! I already told you that's no good!"
PARENT: "The second choice is that you hire a professional chaperone. You can call the police department and they will give you some referrals. Or, you may know some adults who would meet our approval."
TEEN: "Oh, fine! That's even worse."
PARENT: "The third choice is that you can wait and have that unsupervised party at your own home after you go out on your own."
TEEN: "This is stupid. Can't you think of anything better?"
PARENT: "That's the best we can do. Maybe you can think of something better. Let us know what you decide."
TEEN: "No!!! I told you what I want!"
PARENT: "You know the choices. Let us know what you decide."
TEEN: "This house is a police state. I can't wait to move out."
PARENT: "We love you too much to argue with you about it. Let us know what you decide."

These wise parents, when confronted with a problem they weren't expecting, relied on the two rules of Love and Logic. They took good care of themselves by avoiding the arguing. They also gave the problem back to the teenager in the form of choices.

© 1999 Jim Fay

VOLUME

15

"I'll Show You!"

By Jim Fay

VOL. 15, NO. 1

I sat at the table in an airport coffee shop biding my time until departure. I was tired and anxious to get home, but the minutes ticked away in the dull atmosphere. My mind wandered as I sank into the gloom of trying to pass time, too tired to read or work.

Suddenly alert, it occurred to me that the scene before me had brightened considerably. It became obvious that the glow came from the excited face of the young cashier. The reason for her excitement was the approach of her friend. In no time at all, the excitement of the two teenagers illuminated the scene like a torch.

"Oh, you did it," chirped the cashier. "Do you like it? This is so cool!"

"Yeah, I finally did it. It's great! I've had it for two days now."

I realized that all this joy and excitement was about the friend's recently pierced tongue and new gold tongue ring. I had a hard time not cringing when I thought of the pain this girl had subjected herself to.

The two girls were now face to face, leaning on the counter and talking in low voices that made it hard for me to eavesdrop to the extent that I wished. But I did notice that the excitement had died down considerably and that both girls had entered a more somber, depressed state.

Being a student of childhood behavior, I was especially intrigued with the situation and did my best to listen to their conversation. I was able to catch bits and pieces of their discussion. I was especially tuned in when the friend admitted, "It still hurts real bad and I can't swallow solid food."

Suddenly her face lit up again as she remembered why she had subjected herself to all that pain in the first place. With a sly grin, she announced, "But it's so great. My dad is so pissed! He's really losing it this time!"

I asked myself, "What kind of relationship do this girl and her father have that would encourage these kinds of actions? What basic need does this child have that is not being met?"

Basic Human Needs

All humans have basic needs that include:

• Love and affection
• Control
• Inclusion (being an important member of a group)

When these needs are not being met or they are being met in an unhealthy way, we can expect to see negative behaviors or acting out. These behaviors have to do with the person's attempts to get the needs met in other ways or trying to let others know that the needs are not being met.

Thinking about this girl's statement about her dad, we can make some educated guesses about the degree to which her basic needs are being met. Does she feel loved and appreciated by her dad? I doubt it. Healthy people don't usually purposely try to irritate or antagonize those people who offer true love and affection.

We also can make an educated guess as to whether her control needs are being met in a healthy way. We can guess that Dad is either extremely controlling, or at the other end of the scale, providing no limits or boundaries.

In our experience, we often have seen that kids are willing even to hurt themselves if they think it will lead to getting their control needs met.

Parenting with Love and Logic was designed to help parents raise the odds that their children will not have to resort to such extremes to get their basic needs met. Built into the philosophy and techniques offered through Love and Logic are the kinds of parent behaviors and actions that provide for healthy achievement of feelings of:

- Love and affection
- Control
- Inclusion

Kids who grow up with Love and Logic parents are frequently making many of their own decisions within firm, reasonable limits. They are given many opportunities to make mistakes and learn from the consequences. Their childhood mistakes bring about consequences with empathy instead of parental anger and criticism. They feel a sense of love and control rather than rejection.

Kids in Love and Logic families make contributions to the family in the form of chores so they can feel like an important and needed part of the family group.

Many of these kids are responsible for preparing and serving one family meal per week. They can say, with pride, to their friends, "I have to be home. It's my night to cook for the family." They feel needed and appreciated.

Instead of developing internal voices that say, "If I do something wrong, my parents will really be mad," kids who grow up in Love and Logic homes develop internal voices that keep reminding them, "I wonder how much pain and grief I am going to cause myself with my next decision?"

What are the odds that a youngster who grows up with this kind of thinking would find herself resorting to the extreme behaviors of the girl in this story?

© 1999 Jim Fay

CLINE'S CORNER

When Bad Things Happen in Good Families: Handling Grief and Illness

By Foster W. Cline, M.D.

VOL. 15, NO. 1

There is one great hopeful truth about kids in pain. Most of it goes away no matter what we do. But accurate assessment of the pain, particularly if it is chronic, is essential.

I well remember John, who was brought in by his mom because he had bellyaches nearly every morning just before the school bus came. John's pediatrician had diagnosed the problem as a manifestation of school phobia and sent John to me.

John described his pain to me—it was lower right quadrant pain. I had him lie down the floor, then I pressed on the area where he said he had pain. From his responses, and the tightness of the area, I thought there was a very good chance he had appendicitis—chronic, verging on acute—and recommended he go back to the pediatrician who originally had referred John to me.

As is so often the case, John and his mom never returned, and I didn't know what the outcome had been. Eventually the whole episode slipped from my mind.

Years later I ran into a woman who stayed after a presentation to talk with me. It was John's mom, and she laughingly reminded me of the visit. By then John was in college. He had an appendectomy on the day after I saw him so many years before! And his pain had *never* recurred.

There are some truths about childhood pain:

- When children are in psychological pain, they feel it in their bodies. Adult figures-of-speech come from these childhood realities. "He gives me a headache" or "What a pain in the gut" or "Makes you want to throw up" and other slightly more vulgar figures-of-speech are all acted out or truly physically felt in childhood.
- Children may feel gut pain more acutely than adults. Although it is difficult to gauge accurately the "amount of pain" a per-

son may feel, many think that in children the average bellyache does hurt relatively more than in adults.

- Certain people, for largely unknown reasons, mature into adulthood still feeling psychological pain as physical pain. I have found that these people, like children, have a very hard time talking out feelings. They *feel* them physically. Carried to extremes this is called hypochondriasis.

The rules for handling childhood pain:

- Always take the child's complaint seriously, just as we would want our complaints taken seriously.
- Show your child that you are concerned but not alarmed about the situation. If you are a faith-filled person, let the child know it. If there is any doubt about the physical nature of the pain, get a medical opinion. If you are uncertain or unsatisfied with the opinion you receive, ask for a second opinion.

All *good* physicians encourage second opinions. They do not take their patient's desire for a second opinion personally and they do not feel a lack of trust. Most of us simply realize we are dealing with a wise person, who on a critical matter wants to cover the bases.

Parents often wonder how they should handle their child's illness or the serious illness of siblings. There are some rules:

- Always be truthful. I have found over the years that children often handle their life-threatening illnesses *much* better than the parents. At the same time, always be hopeful about the future.
- Generally, children handle tough situations about as well as the adults in the environment. Children model their behavior on how adults handle tough times. If parents are worried and wringing their hands, so are the children. If the adults are silent and brave, so are the children.
- Occasionally a child uses a sad situation, or a difficult happening, to become overly distraught. They are overreacting to a

situation the adults are handling well. When this happens it is not helpful to tell the child to straighten up, buck up, or quit crying. (None of those approaches works with spouses, either!)

It is best for parents to use the Love and Logic principle of putting themselves first in a loving way and saying to the child, "Honey, I know you are really upset about this, and I can understand that. However, I don't like your hassling my eardrums about it so strongly, because that could bring me down and make me even sadder. So if you want to wail, pitch a fit, or cry about it, you need to do it someplace else. Thank you."

For many years, if it fits with their belief system, I have advised parents to handle death's reality this way:

- Light a candle. Tell the child that the flame is like the spark in a person's eyes, the smile, their "life force" or soul—use words with which you are comfortable. Light another candle from the first and blow out the first. Take the second candle and place it out of sight.
- Tell the child, "Now, when a person dies, it is like this first candle is the body. It doesn't light up anymore. The spark and shine are gone. Just the part that carried the flame is left, but it is not too interesting. It is exciting that the flame still burns. It's just as bright. You can't see it, but it has been transferred to a spot beyond our vision. But it's there.

  "And like this candle, your brother's spark, his smile, the light in his eyes are now out of sight. And tomorrow when we go to the funeral, it's as if we will be saying goodbye to this old candlestick. We liked the candlestick, and we got used to it, but its purpose was simply to carry the flame until it could be transferred to burn forever in another place."

In summary, it is most important to realize that children take their point of view from the adults in the environment. All of life is filtered through the parents' perceptions.

So, on all issues, parents need to set the model for how they would like and expect their child to handle the situation. If the child is not handling the situation in a healthy way, first talk over the situation and do problem-solving. If that doesn't bring the child relief, tell the child he or she will need to spend a little time getting it together elsewhere.

Parents need to be understanding, available, and giving, but they need not put up with a child who is overly distraught after other methods of relieving the problem have failed.

Love and Logic House Rules
By Jim Fay
VOL. 15, NO. 2

Okay, kids, I've had it! That does it! We're going to have some rules around here!

This declaration probably was issued thousands of times last week in homes across America. My guess is that many of those rules already have been broken and/or abandoned.

Having and enforcing rules in the home is important. Constantly adding new rules each time the old ones are broken instead of consistently enforcing existing rules often leads to more chaos and frustration in a family.

I once worked with a school that had fallen into the trap of trying to have a specific rule to cover everything a student might do. At this school, a boy brought a dead fish into the classroom and slapped a girl with it. The teacher immediately told him that this kind of behavior was against the rules.

"Oh, no, it's not," he countered. "I've read all 314 of the rules at this school, and there's not one rule about a dead fish."

Quick to recover, the school personnel made up another rule to cover this situation. Alas, it didn't solve the problem. Two weeks later the same student was sent to the office for violating the "no slapping kids with dead fish rule." He arrived in the assistant principal's office with an encyclopedia in hand.

"I don't know why I'm in trouble this time," he insisted. "It says right on this page in the encyclopedia that salamanders are not fish. The rule only says fish."

I'm sure of two things. This youngster is headed for a great career in the legal field, and the school never can win by making rules so specific.

My advice for schools and families is the same. Have a limited number of rules that are both enforceable and global in nature. If this school had had a rule that stated, "Be prepared to solve any problem you make for others," it would have been easy for the teacher to tell the student that his behavior made a problem for others. There would have been no need to argue over the difference between fish and salamanders.

Rules for Rules

1. Know how you are going to enforce the rule before you make the rule.

A parent who makes a rule such as, "No watching TV while I'm gone," has a problem. If the child knows there is no way the rule can be enforced, he starts viewing his parent as all mouth and no action. He starts thinking to himself, "My parent is a paper tiger. I probably don't have to follow any of the other rules either." This leads to a lot of testing of limits by the child.

2. Make the rule global in nature.

Each rule needs to be stated in a way that causes it to include all eventualities. When we fail to state rules this way, it leads children to practice arguing and hair-splitting. For example, a parent who makes a rule that says, "No throwing things in the house," is often confronted with a creative kid who is kicking his ball in the house instead. Not only is there still a problem, there is a second problem as well, called arguing.

"Geez! I'm not throwing anything. You said no throwing. Why are you always on my case? I never get to do anything. Besides, I'm not hurting anything!"

Rules for the Love and Logic Home
The following rules are the ones that have served Love and Logic parents best. They are both enforceable and global.

Rule 1: Treat your parents with the same respect with which they treat you. It would be natural for a thoughtful person to ask, "Wait a minute. How can we control what comes out of the mouths of others?" The truth is that we can't. Parents can't control whether their children are respectful, but they can enforce the rule. Enforcing this rule may require the parents to go on strike until the child behaves in a respectful way.

Instead of telling back-talking kids to show a little respect, Love and Logic parents say, "I'm not feeling respected. I'll have to deal with that, but not right now." At this point the parent goes on strike, waiting with wild anticipation for the next time the child needs something.

The way parents go on strike is to announce, "I will be happy to do the things you need me to do when I feel treated with respect."

When the youngster says, "When are you going to wash my clothes?" the parent answers, "I'll be happy to do the things you need when I feel treated with respect."

When the youngster asks, "Will you drive me to my game?" the parent says, "I'll be happy to do the things you need when I feel treated with respect."

Rule 2: Everybody in the house does his or her fair share of the work. One of the foundation blocks of a successful, happy life is a sense of belonging and importance to the family. We often see hostile, unhappy kids who are also apathetic about their studies.

When analyzing the family structure we find that these kids are treated like guests in a five-star hotel. They want for nothing and they make no contributions to the family in the form of doing their fair share of the work. Their parents often are heard saying, "I can't understand this. I've given this kid everything he's ever wanted and he's still nasty."

This rule is one of the easiest to enforce. Refer to the Love and Logic audiotape *"Didn't I Tell You to Take Out the Trash?"* for help. You and your child will both be much happier when you learn how to get the chores done without a battle and without reminders.

Rule 3: Be prepared to solve any problem you make for others. The family understanding is that kids can solve the problem in almost any way, provided the solution does not make a problem for anyone else on the planet. This rule can cover a wide range of issues, from draining the parent's energy with arguing and talking back to major problems such as drinking, stealing, violence, etc. Many Love and Logic parents have found this rule especially helpful when they find themselves needing to deal with situations they don't feel prepared to handle.

These parents are quick to say, "Wow. I'm not sure how I want to handle this right now. I'll get back to you on it." In the event that a parent can't identify a logical consequence, they fall back on having the child pay restitution for the parent's time and energy spent working on the problem.

A parent using this technique would say, "I spent a lot of time trying to figure out what I was going to do about your constant begging yesterday. What I was going to do instead was sweep the driveway. Unfortunately I can't do two things at once, so as soon as you get that job done for me, we can call it even. Thanks."

Rule 4: Be prepared, at eighteen years of age, to continue your education or to be totally self-supporting. As a child, I carried this message in my head. Not for one minute did I think that my parents were going to support me after I graduated from high school. I also knew from day one that the only support my parents would be capable of giving me with my education was allowing me to live at home while I went to college.

I knew that this did not have to do with their love, but it was all they could do with their meager income.

How did my parents get me to carry and accept this message without feeling resentful? They started talking about it when I was very young. They told their friends when I could overhear their conversations.

It never occurred to me that things might be any different. When I asked how I was supposed to earn enough to afford college, they responded with, "There are lots of ways of getting an education and part of it is being smart enough to ask questions and figure it out for yourself." Guess what? I did.

If, by chance, your youngster has grown up with the belief that his parents are supposed to provide a comfortable life at their expense after high school, help is on its way.

I have produced a prototype letter you can copy in your own handwriting. It will change this situation. It is written so that all your love will show through as you send your youngster out into the world to be a self-supporting adult.

You can find the letter in an article titled "When It's Time for Them to Get a Life." It can be found on page 99 of *The Love and Logic Journal Tenth Anniversary Collection.*

The Delayed or "Anticipatory" Consequence: What to Do When You Don't Know What to Do
By Charles Fay, Ph.D.

Vol. 15, No. 2

Have you ever found yourself stumped by something your kid has said or done? Have you ever found yourself thinking rather sarcastically, "Oh great! What in the world am I going to do this time?"

And has a little voice ever whispered in your ear, "Yell at that kid! Come on, let him have it! Ground him for life!"?

If you answered yes to any of these questions, *you are normal!* Recently, a parent called me and described a situation in which her teenage son refused to do his chores.

After he was asked very nicely to vacuum the rug, he became righteously indignant and said, "My friends don't have to do that stuff. I'm not doing it. I'm not your slave." Then he walked out of the room with his nose in the air.

Similarly, a teacher wrote me and described how one of her students yelled a rather vulgar comment having to do with the behavior of another child's mother. She said the entire class looked up from their books and said, "Ooooooooooooo."

What's a parent or teacher to do? According to some psychologists and mental health professionals, we must respond with an *immediate* consequence. That is, one never should allow an extended period of time to occur between a child's misbehavior and a well-reasoned, logical consequence.

Although this theory may sound good on paper, it often fails miserably in the testing grounds of real life. Why? One reason has to do with how difficult it is to think of an immediate consequence when the "heat is on."

Frequently, I ask audiences of parents, teachers, and mental health professionals to raise their hands if they are good at thinking of logical consequences in response to their children's misbehavior. I see very few hands.

Nevertheless, during a recent presentation a woman raised her hand and said, "I usually can't think of a good consequence, but I sure can think of what I'd like to do to him." Then she smiled, "But I don't think that's legal!"

A second problem with the "immediate consequences" theory is that parents and teachers often report being too angry or frustrated to use enforceable consequences. The term "enforceable consequence" refers to a consequence that we can actually pull off or enforce.

Too frequently, we feel pressure to provide an immediate consequence, feel frustrated or angry, and then say something we can't back up in a million years.

Recently I heard a mother do this in a local park. Turning to her two misbehaving boys, she yelled, "All right! That's it! You're grounded for three weeks! You can forget about leaving the house, and don't think about watching TV either!"

Unfortunately, this type of "consequence" is more of a punishment for the mother than her sons. And what are the chances she will back down when they begin to make her life miserable at home? The sad result of using such unenforceable consequences or "threats" is that our children soon learn we don't really mean what we say.

Lastly, immediate consequences are generally very hard to apply without anger. At the heart of Love and Logic is the principle that consequences must be delivered with empathy or sadness for the child. When this sadness is "locked in" before the consequence is delivered, three very valuable things happen.

First, the child experiences sadness as a result of disappointing a loving authority figure. Second, the child is forced to "own" his or her pain instead of blaming it on the adult's anger. Third, a positive adult–child relationship is maintained.

When these three conditions are in place, consequences are more powerful, and children tend to gain a great deal of wisdom from their mistakes. In contrast, when consequences are delivered with anger, children often are forced to repeat the same painful mistakes over and over.

If immediate, logical consequences are so difficult to apply effectively, what can we do instead? Let's take a look at an alternative technique initially developed by Jim Fay and termed the "delayed consequence."

With this technique, the consequence is delayed just long enough for the adult to calm down and develop a plan in which a logical consequence can be delivered with sincere empathy. The length of delay depends on the "mental" age of the child.

This delay may range from an hour for a child functioning at a two-year-old level, to a few hours or overnight for a child functioning at four years of age, to a week for an intelligent teenager.

Let's take a closer look at how the mother mentioned earlier used this technique. When she asked her teenage son to vacuum, and he said, "I'm not doing it ... I'm not your slave," she walked over to him, raised her eyebrows, and whispered, "This is really sad. I'm going to have to do something about this ... but ... I think I'll wait until I talk to my friends and come up with something really good ... Try not to worry about it."

His eyes lit up as he asked, "What are you gonna do?"

She repeated, "Try not to worry."

He tried again, "Come on. What are you gonna do?"

Walking away, she once again repeated, "Try not to worry about it."

What are the chances that this kid is really "worrying about it"? Does Mom have some time to calm down, talk to her friends, and develop a strong and logical consequence she can apply with sadness instead of anger?

And does she now have some time to predict how her son might react and to get prepared for this reaction?

Recently I changed the name of this technique to the "anticipatory consequence," because delaying the consequence is only a small part of what really takes place. In addition, this technique forces the child to "anticipate" or worry about what might happen, and it allows the adult to "anticipate" or spend time determining how to apply a logical and enforceable consequence without anger.

In this particular example, Mom took some time to calm down and to think. The next day, her son came running out of his room. "Mom! Somebody stole the new CD player you bought me!"

Mom responded with sadness. "Oh no. I pawned it."

"What are you talking about?!" he screamed.

"I love you too much to fight with you about doing the housework, so I decided to hire someone else to do it and pay them with the money from your CD player. I sold it to Uncle Steve, but if you hurry, you might be able to buy it back from him before he decides to keep it."

This technique can be applied in the classroom, too! Let's take a closer look at how the teacher mentioned earlier used an anticipatory consequence with a student "talking trash" about another kid's mother.

In this example, the teacher slowly walked over to the student, raised her eyebrows, and whispered sadly, "Oh, bummer. I'm going to have to do something about this ... but not now ... later ... Try not to worry about it."

Again, the student reacted with, "What are you gonna do?"

Again, the adult whispered while walking away, "Try not to worry."

Next, the teacher talked to the school principal, and both of them developed a plan with help from the student's mother. Just before school ended that afternoon, the student was called to the office.

There he found his teacher, the principal, and his mother. His mother looked at him and said with sincere sadness, "This is sad—a two-day suspension. Let me know how you plan to pay for the baby-sitter who will be watching you, and the gasoline and time I burned dealing with this problem."

Use of the anticipatory consequence technique provides a healthy and practical alternative to reacting immediately, because it allows all parties to calm down, forces the child to anticipate a wide array of possible consequences, and enables the adult to develop a plan and gain needed support from others.

Despite these benefits, some argue that research in learning theory clearly discourages delaying consequences. In other words, this research indicates that consequences *must* be provided immediately or the child will not make a clear association between the misbehavior and the consequence.

Taking a more careful look at this research, as well as our anticipatory consequence technique, one realizes that this strategy provides the best of both worlds—the benefits of both immediate and delayed consequencing!

To understand how this happens, it's helpful to do some time travel back to the late 1800s. At this time, a Russian physiologist named Ivan Pavlov was hard at work studying the chemical makeup of dog saliva or "dog spit." In his passion for drool, Ivan devised a method by which he could collect these juices by directly attaching tubes to his canine friends' salivary glands.

When he walked into his laboratory and placed meat in front of the dogs, saliva ran down these tubes, collecting in basins below. Before long, Ivan made one of the most influential discoveries in modern psychology.

To his surprise, the dogs began to salivate each time he walked into the lab—even when he was without the meat. From this observation, he realized that the dogs had come to associate his appearance with the meat.

He began to experiment and realized that if he rang a bell each time before presenting the meat, the dogs soon would begin to salivate to the sound of the bell alone (Pavlov, 1927)!

With the anticipatory consequence technique, the same type of basic conditioning takes place. Instead of ringing a bell before presenting meat, we are saying, "Try not to worry about it" before presenting a logical consequence.

As a result of this conditioning, children soon begin to associate logical consequences with "Try not to worry about it." In other words, "Try not to worry about it" becomes a consequence in and of itself—a consequence that can be effectively delivered immediately after an instance of misbehavior.

Another objection to the use of this technique has to do with the amount of time taking place between "Try not to worry about it" and the logical consequence.

Early behavioral researchers believed that conditioning would take place only if the actual or "unconditioned" consequence (i.e., the meat) was preceded immediately by the learned or "conditioned" event (i.e., the bell).

More recently, researchers have realized that the amount of time between these two events is not as important as how well the first predicts the second (Rescorla, 1988). That is, the amount of time that passes after "Try not to worry about it" is not as important as whether the adult always walks over to the child within an hour, day, or week (depending on the child's mental age) and says something like, "Remember when I said I was going to do something about the holes you made in the wall? Remember when I said I was going to give it some thought first? Well, I decided not to argue with you about it. I'll be happy to start giving you allowance again after I have enough money to fix the damage. This should be about two months, unless you decide to do some extra jobs to pay it off faster."

References

Pavlov, I.P. (1927). *Conditioned reflexes*. New York: Oxford University Press.

Rescorla, R.A. (1988). Pavlovian conditioning: It's not what you think it is. *American Psychologist, 43*, 151–160.

CLINE'S CORNER

On Kids Killing Kids:
How Do We React with Our Children?
By Foster W. Cline, M.D.

VOL. 15, No. 2

Everyone is concerned about the tragedy in Littleton, Colorado. And there are going to be more such trials ahead.

No one can realistically think that the few dozens of children who have been killed in schools the last few years will be the last to be gunned down on the playground or in the library. There will be many more.

Copycat crimes are numerous, and our own local high school has had four or five free days because of bomb threats in the past few weeks. Across the country, I am sure there are thousands of students who, considering themselves lucky, have had many spring days off because of bomb threats.

How Do We Address These Issues with Our Kids?

First, with our children, we need to keep things in perspective. Their chances of dying in a car accident far exceed their chances of being gunned down in school. Their chances of dying from an infection exceed their chances of being killed in school.

Of the hundreds of thousands of schools in the United States, a handful have had problems. Of the thousands of children attending high schools, only a few have been disturbed. So if you have a child who insists on worrying about something, in a loving, slightly light manner, tell him or her to worry about what really counts and focus on car accidents.

Remember that children generally handle crises about as well as the adults in the environment. Children learn by modeling. When bad things happen, hand-wringing parents raise terrified children, angry parents raise angry children, and thoughtful, concerned parents who are not too bent out of shape raise children who stand pretty straight themselves.

Finally, try as much as possible to stick to the facts of the situation. It is probably a situation that doesn't need a lot of editorializing by parents, but does need to be explored:

> "How do you feel about the problems at Columbine?" (If you already have talked with your child about how you *feel* about it, don't bother; you will just hear your own feelings fed back to you.)
> "Have you felt scared at school?"
> "How do you handle situations where you are worried?" (Don't buy trouble—he or she may never have been worried!)
> "What can you do to best ensure that nothing like this happens at your school?"

What Are the Signs That Your Child May Become Dangerous to Himself or Others?

* First, almost every suicidal or homicidal child talks about committing the act before he or she does it. Usually there is someone who is *not* surprised by the act of homicide or suicide.

  Parents (and friends) often respond with, "Oh, you don't mean that!" or "It'll work out," when they should *explore and understand rather than reassure*. The questions to ask, again without being too bent out of shape (do it like a therapist would), are:

"How long have you felt that way?"

"Do you think it is getting better or worse?"

"What are the disadvantages and advantages for you of ____?"

And provide realistic *hope* for the child. If the child does not seem to feel significantly better after talking or if you have any doubts at all, seek professional consultation.

• Danger signs of depression and hopelessness in a child with high self-esteem could include sudden changes:

Reclusive behavior.

Change in friends.

Drop in grades.

Decrease in personal care and hygiene.

Acting like he or she has a chip on his or her shoulder.

Outbursts of rage.

Loss of long-term friends.

Complaints of feeling like a failure.

Giving away favorite possessions.

• Any behavior that gives one a feeling that the child is feeling hopeless ("Everybody hates me anyway"), helpless ("There is nothing I can ever do about it"), and angry ("I'd like to kill them") are danger signals.

However, keep in mind that these danger signals and the list above may all occur with children who never would commit suicide or homicide. And they occur for other reasons: when children start abusing drugs or in cases of the onset of major adolescent psychiatric problems such as bipolar illness.

How Do We Best Suicide- and Homicide-Proof Our Kids?

Kids who kill themselves and others always feel helpless and hopeless. They lack the internal resources to cope.

Although great parenting techniques can best ensure a child has good coping skills, the best of parents may occasionally raise a homicidal or suicidal youth. When a youth commits suicide or homicide:

It is not the fault of the parents.
It is not the fault of the gun manufacturers.
It is not the fault of the teachers or principals.
It is not the fault of the therapists.
It is not the fault of TV, movies, or video games.

The murdering children themselves had a big problem. Don't ever let your own kids off the hook by blaming their behavior on things outside their skin. That is how children are taught *not* to cope.

Anything that decreases personal accountability and responsibility decreases coping skills, and there is a *lot* of that going on in our country. In fact, the lack of personal accountability and responsibility play a far greater role in societal mayhem than the availability of guns.

Guns have always been available. And kids didn't always shoot kids. If and when guns are banned, kids will still, as they do in England, kill kids with bombs and knives in a society where no one is accountable or responsible for his or her decisions and actions.

To best suicide- and homicide-proof your children, raise them with the Love and Logic techniques found every month in this *Journal.* Give them love, affection, time, choices, and above all, give them empathy when you allow them to *suffer* the consequences of their behavior.

Help them cope with consequences when things go wrong, and don't rescue them from hard times. You will raise children who can cope. And helplessness and hopelessness probably will not be a part of their repertoire.

© 1999 Foster W. Cline, M.D.

"Teaseproof" Your Kids
By Jim Fay
VOL. 15, NO. 3

Mom, I don't want to go to school. It's not fair. Mrs. Taylor tells the kids not to tease me, but they still do it when she's not watching 'em. I try to ignore 'em just like you said, but they just do it all the more.

Loving parents who are confronted with this feel like a piece of their heart is being ripped out. What a hopeless feeling we have when our kids are being rejected or teased by other kids. It is not uncommon at these times to have feelings that include both heartache and rage.

We think to ourselves, "Why can't the school people protect my child? Don't they realize that we put our kids in their hands, and therefore our trust?"

The sad truth is that the more a teacher protects the child who is teased, the more resentful and aggressive the other children become. A teacher who tells kids to be nice to a specific child actually "marks" that youngster and sets him/her up for more intense rejection and ridicule.

When it comes to teasing, the only person who can protect your child from teasing is your child. Kids have some sort of built-in sonar that causes them to zero in on certain kids, and they can be unmerciful in their torment.

Watching this happen can be a gut-wrenching experience for any adult. But the good news is that we can actually help kids become "teaseproof."

Have you ever noticed that some kids never get teased while others are constantly subjected to teasing? There is a pattern to this.

Kids who are never teased never worry about being teased. They can't imagine that it would ever happen to them. They have an aura around them that says, "I can handle myself!"

Kids who do get teased constantly worry about being ridiculed and send out nonverbal messages that indicate lack of confidence and fear of teasing. Children are especially in tune with nonverbal signals of weakness. Without realizing what they are doing, they zero in on these kids. Two subconscious goals come into play. The first is, "I can show others that I am superior to that kid," and the other is, "That kid's weak and I better show him that he needs to toughen up."

Remember that none of this happens at the conscious level. It just happens and appears to be human nature.

The trick to "teaseproofing" a youngster is giving him/her the skills to be able to handle teasing. Once the child realizes they can actually handle the problem, you will see a change in the nonverbal attitude. The other kids will recognize this and start looking for different targets.

Mr. Mendez, a wonderful second-grade teacher, "teaseproofed" his whole class. He said to the class, "Kids, the reason kids tease other kids is that it makes them feel superior. Now you can let them get away with this or you can use an adult one-liner. But first of all, we all have to practice the 'cool look.'"

This teacher had the kids practice standing with their hands in their pockets, rocking back on their heels, and putting a cool grin on their face.

He practiced this over and over. Every now and then, he would yell out, "Let's see your 'cool look.'" The kids would all jump out of their seats and put on the "look."

Once they had all mastered the "cool look," he said, "When kids start to tease you, put on your 'cool look.' Keep the look going while they tease. As soon as they get through putting you down, use your one-liner."

The one-liner he taught them is one of the famous Love and Logic one-liners: "Thanks for sharing that with me." Mr. Mendez had the kids practice this, making sure that they kept the "cool look" on while they said the words.

Every now and then, when the kids would least expect it, he would yell out, "Let me hear your one-liner!" And the kids would practice saying the words, making sure to grin while they said them.

Once the teacher felt that the class had mastered saying, "Thanks for sharing that with me," in the appropriate way, he started having them practice jumping up out of their seats, putting on the "cool look," and saying their one-liner.

The next step was for the kids to learn to turn around on the last word and walk away fast without looking back at the teasing child. Needless to say, they all did their practice until the skill was mastered. They even spent some of their recess time practicing this on the playground.

Now that the skill was learned, practiced, and mastered, Mr. Mendez could implement his part of the operation. When children came to him to tattle about others teasing them, he consistently asked, "Did you let him get by with it or did you use your 'cool skill'?"

In the event that child admitted that they had not used their skill, the teacher said, "How sad that you let him get by with it. Do you suppose you are going to continue to let him get by with it or are you going to use your skill? It's your choice, but tattling to me is no longer a choice."

Mr. Mendez tells us that the amount of tattling and complaining has been reduced by over 90 percent. He also proudly tells about one of his students who came to him asking if they had to use the one-liner he taught him, or could they make up their own.

This second-grader wanted to demonstrate to the class the one-liner that he used so successfully on the playground.

He stood before the class and said, "This other kid on the playground was dissin' me. He said I had the skinniest arms in the whole school. I put on my 'cool look,' I grinned, and said, 'Bummer, I thought I was cool, man.' I walked away before he could figure out what to say. Man, I blew his mind!"

All the kids clapped for this skillful second-grader, and the teacher beamed with pride as he thought to himself, "Now that kid is really 'teaseproof' for sure."

You don't have to wait for the teacher to "teaseproof" your kids. You can do it in your home the same way Mr. Mendez did in the classroom. What a gift you can give your child, and come to think of it, what a gift it is to a parent to know that we can send our kids out into the world "teaseproof."

Since the development of the "cool look" skill, many different kids have found sanctuary in its use. One of the most creative applications was seen at a local school where the kids seem to take great pleasure in claiming to do research on the behavior of other kids' mothers and attacking each other with this information when they are mad.

One kid yelled out to the other, "Yo momma's a ho!" The youngster being attacked put on his "cool look" and retorted, "I tell her to be nice, but she gets mad when I tell her what to do." With this he turned and walked away.

The teacher who witnessed this reported that the attacker's mouth fell open and all he could say under his breath was, "Man, that guy's weird. He be weird."

Now the kid who pulled this one off is absolutely "teaseproof." Even if kids try to tease him, the attacks will bounce off like Ping-Pong balls off a stone wall.

© 1999 Jim Fay

A Foster Cline Q & A Session
VOL. 15, No. 3

Question

My preschooler still wants the pacifier. At what age should this stop?

Answer

Professionally, I am not much of a believer in pacifiers in the first place. I think right from the beginning, during critical times of brain development, they lock in connections that essentially tell a child, "Get frustrated, get bored, get fussy, and feel better by putting something in your mouth."

I do think *infants* may feel better with a nipple in their mouths pretty continuously, but toddlers, no. The reason pacifiers are bad in toddlerhood is that they are isolating for the child. For instance, when one sees a toddler walking around with a pacifier in his or her mouth, only the kid's mother thinks it is cute. Most adults won't even say hello to the kid, and men, more than women, I have found, immediately look another direction.

Once a child gets used to a pacifier, it is hard at times to wean him or her and they can get very demanding. Our daughter had a favorite rabbit that she carried around sucking on its ears, to the point that the rabbit smelled like a sewer, even after being washed! (So creative kids can always find things other than a pacifier to suck on.)

We solved the problem by progressively clipping the rabbit's moldy ears shorter and shorter until, "Look at that, Honey, all gone! The rabbit has molted its ears!"

I think if a toddler wants a pacifier at night, that is great.

I think that parents may have a hard time getting a kid to *quit* sucking on something, but they can start to control *where* it happens. This is much more effective:

PARENT: "Honey, it looks like you are into sucking your finger (your thumb, your pacifier, etc.) right now. And I'm sure it feels good to you. But it is a hassle to my eyeballs, so I need you to do it up in your room, and when you get it out of your system in fifteen minutes or so, join us."

Children soon learn that when they behave in a way that hassles others, they will be asked politely, with consideration, and *without* parental frustration, to leave the area, for a given length of time.

Learning this, they usually quit doing the self-destructive behavior, whatever it may be. When they are asked to leave, it must be for much longer than one minute per year of age!

• • •

Question

My child ends up in frustration when it's past bedtime and his homework is not finished. When should he do it? Right after school seems too demanding with no rest in between school and homework.

Answer

The problem is very clear here. You are concerned and worried about what he should do and he probably knows it. These are the everyday decisions that we all have to make. Should I sit down at the computer and answer this question, or should I go skiing on the last beautiful day that the lift is running? Should I relax after work or get right into writing my new book? Your question is akin exactly to someone saying, "My husband is frustrated because his dictation is not being done on a timely basis for the hospital medical records personnel; however, he is tired when he gets home. What can we do?"

Let's play this out first with an ineffective parent:

MOM: "Honey, isn't watching TV at 4:00 a little early? Don't you have homework?"

KID: "Yeah, but I'm tired!"

MOM: "Well you need to get it done before bedtime."

KID: "I will ..."

MOM: (five hours later) "It's bedtime."

KID: "I gotta do my homework!"

MOM: "Well, it's after bedtime and you need your sleep."

KID: "I need to do it before tomorrow."

MOM: "Well, you can get up early and do it."

KID: "I don't want to get up early."

And on *ad infinitum*. It is not pleasant. The kid "yes, buts" all solutions and ends up frustrated and angry in the parents' presence and the parents feel helpless and frustrated themselves.

Now let's look at this being handled effectively:

MOM: "Geez, watching TV at 4:00 in the afternoon? Hope your brain doesn't shrivel!"

KID: "Yeah, but I like this program and it's relaxing after school."

MOM: "Great! See you at dinnertime."

Mom doesn't mention homework, as it is none of her business. Or, if she is raising a kid who really can't get his own act together, she might set the model, be a good example, and wonder about when he'll get the homework done, saying, "You're lucky you can relax when you still have work to do. That's always been hard for me. I can never seem to really relax until my jobs are done."

Now the kid is faced with choices and the consequences of poor decisions:

- Stay up all night and do homework (and be asked to leave others' presence the next day if he is snarky from lack of sleep).
- Snap off the TV and do it now (which leads the mother to say, "That's probably wise").
- Get up very early and do the homework.
- Not do the homework.
- Plead poor planning with the teacher and see if she'll be understanding and let him do it on the weekend. (Only a teacher who is a *real* pushover would agree to this!)

The child can carry out any or all of the above feeling, or not feeling, frustration.

The only thing the parent is required to do is to set a good model and let the child know beyond a shadow of a doubt that he *can't* hassle the parent with his frustration.

This is a happy home! People are allowed to be angry and frustrated with themselves but are not allowed to take it out on others!

For example:

KID: "I'm going to have to stay up all night now and get my homework done."

PARENT: "Looks like it."

KID: "And it's just not fair!"

PARENT: "I can understand your feeling that way."

KID: "And will you help me?"

PARENT: "Dream on. I'm the type of person who needs my sleep."

KID: "Well, it just isn't fair!"

PARENT: "Probably! Good night, Honey."

• • •

Question

What do you think is the right age for first-time field trips that require flying? Also, mission trips to Third World countries—what age is okay?

Answer

I am assuming all the trips and all the flights are scheduled by responsible people or organizations. With responsible children, whenever the children themselves think they are ready for something, they should be given the opportunity to learn from failure or success.

With irresponsible kids, whenever the parent thinks the kid is ready is the right time. Flying per se is not a problem.

Little kids fly without their parents all the time and are shepherded on and off planes by flight attendants. Any kid that can ride a bus or take a cab by himself can fly and be met at the destination airport by relatives or friends.

The real issue is the age requirements set by the airline.

Concerning mission trips, it's hard to say. I've been a youth leader and I know of ten-year-olds who would be a help and get a lot out of a mission trip for a few weeks to South America. And I know of sixteen-year-olds whom you couldn't pay me to take. So make your decision based on the maturity of your child's answers to the following questions:

"Why do you want to go?"

"How will you pay for all (or part) of it?"

"How do you intend to conduct yourself?"

"Why would this be a good learning experience for you?"

"What are the possible drawbacks to going?"

"Are you prepared to pay for your trip home if you are caught smoking, being noncompliant, being less than super helpful, etc.?" (If there is even a *small* chance that the child could be sent home early, then the child has to come up with the return money, to be held in escrow, before leaving on the trip.)

"How would you handle it if there were a kidnapping, the youth leader died, you got an intestinal infection ..." (Sometimes it's nice to know that your child has considered even extreme situations.)

"How will you show us around here that you have both the maturity and the sense of responsibility that proves this trip will be of benefit to you, and your presence a benefit to the youth leader and your host country?" (This need not even be asked of a responsible kid.)

© 1999 Foster W. Cline, M.D.

It's Now Their Problem
By Jim Fay
VOL. 15, NO. 4

Do your kids ever have trouble getting ready to leave for school in the morning? Do they ever make a problem for you as a result?

A very creative mother who attended one of our Love and Logic training sessions came up with this idea. She said that the idea was a direct result of her learning the two rules of Love and Logic.

Telling the group about how she devised her new technique, she said, "The first rule of Love and Logic is that parents set firm limits in loving ways. I learned in class that the trick to this is to tell kids how I intend to take care of myself.

"But the more I analyzed this, the more I discovered that telling kids how I take care of myself is not as powerful as showing them. The more my kids see me taking care of myself, the stronger the limits become."

This mom then went on to tell our group how frustrated she was every morning trying to get her kids ready to leave the house. "I had already been late for work so many times that I was in danger of losing my job. By the time I got those kids in the car and delivered them to school I felt like I had already put in eight hours on the job."

Mom went on to explain that once she learned the second rule of Love and Logic, she was ready to try something new. "I was really turned on to the second rule," she said. "When the instructor told us that when kids cause a problem, we should give the problem back to the kids in a loving way, I thought of a way that getting ready to go in the morning could be the kids' problem instead of mine."

The next Saturday morning, Mom invited the kids to go shopping for some new clothes. Their excitement for shopping was dulled when Mom pulled the car into the parking lot of the local thrift store.

The kids were quick to respond to Mom stopping on the way to their shopping trip. "Why are we stopping here? We don't want to stop here. Can't we do our shopping first? The mall will be crowded if we don't get there early."

"Oh," replied Mom. "We're going to do our shopping here today."

"No way! We don't need the kinds of stuff they sell here. They don't sell designer clothes here. We've already got stuff that's better. This is stupid."

"Yeah," said the oldest girl. "I couldn't be seen in the kind of stuff they sell here. Don't you care about my social life?"

Mom was quick to remind, "That's a pretty arrogant way to talk. There are lots of perfectly good things for sale here. When I was on a tighter budget, I bought quite a few things here. It made sense to me to spend wisely and I got a lot for my money. Let's go in and see what we can find."

"Well, we're not trying on any of these clothes. They're not fashionable. We only wear the latest fashions," reminded the middle child.

Mom was not discouraged by this. She set out to buy a complete outfit for each of the children. Since the kids did not want to try on the clothes, Mom just held them up to each kid to check approximate size.

"I had a great time doing this," laughed Mom. "I made sure to pick the clothes that were the most out-of-style. The more the kids complained, the more fun I had. I was even lucky enough to find some real old sneakers with low tops and thin soles."

"Hey, we're not wearing this stuff. This stuff is gross!"

The more the kids complained, the more Mom realized how spoiled they had become. In the past they had always dictated how she would spend her money. It became evident to her that her kids were going to need some additional lessons about humility after she finished this training session.

This wise mother's response to their rejection of the clothes was, "Not to worry, kids, these clothes are just for emergencies. You may never find a need to wear them, but they will be available."

As soon as Mom got home she put each outfit in a white plastic bag. On each bag she printed, with a bold, black marker: GRAB-AND-GO BAG. The bags were then hung on the doorknob on the entry door.

"Kids, from now on I will not be nagging you to get ready to go in the morning. You will never have to listen to me complaining to you to hurry up.

"I'm sure you can handle getting ready on time. My car will be leaving each morning at 7:45. If you're not dressed and ready, you don't have to worry. Just grab a bag and go. Grab and go! That's all there is to it."

Mom reported to the group that her kids had lived up to their threat of never wearing those out-of-style clothes.

"My mornings are now a pleasure. I get ready. The kids get ready. Now I take all that time I used to spend complaining ... drinking my coffee and listening to the news on television. Life is good again."

The Wonderful World of Wits' End Parenting
By Charles Fay, Ph.D.
VOL. 15, NO. 4

How to Regain Control When Things Get Really Nuts

Wonderful kids can still bring us to our wits' end! When the kids haven't taken the trash out in days, they're fighting like hungry alley cats over the last mouse in town, their favorite response to anything you ask is a whiny, "But why?" and they're reaching "teachers' lounge legend" status at their schools, it's easy to start feeling a bit ... well ... crazy!

A mother came into my office. Her face bore the same recognizable signs I'd seen painted all over many others: bloodshot eyes resting on dark circles, a forehead creased with wrinkles, prematurely gray hair standing on end.

She struggled to find the strength to talk, but once she did, an almost endless flow of frustrations filled the air:

MOM: "Everything has to be a battle with Curtis. Everything I say, he has some sarcastic response to. And then his sister, Amy, jumps in with how she thinks we let him get away with murder. Then they start arguing about who was supposed to feed the dog. And then Curtis just runs off and starts slamming the door."

ME: "So let me see if I've got this right. He argues with you and ..."

MOM: "And did I tell you about Amy's grades? She has so much potential, but all she wants to do is sit around and talk on the phone to her boyfriend. And the school's called three times this month about her brother, too. I mean, why does he constantly have to question everything his teacher says?"

ME: "You're unhappy about her grades."

MOM: "Oh. That reminds me of mornings! Always forgetting their homework. They've made me late so many times I can't tell you."

ME: "So it takes them a long time to get dressed and ..."

MOM: "Yesterday, she came out of the room wearing something—well, I just can't believe what kids these days wear."

There I sat with my Ph.D. in psychology with absolutely no idea of what to say! Panic started to settle in. Where was I supposed to start? Curtis? Amy? Grades? Arguing?

Have you ever felt overwhelmed by the shenanigans your kids pull? Have you ever had brief fantasies about hiring kidnappers? You are not alone!

All parents with kids worth keeping find themselves at wits' end and in need of scream therapy. Those with kids affectionately termed "strong-willed" may find themselves feeling totally out of control more often than not.

How does a parent regain control when problems seem overwhelming? As I sat with this woman in my office, I stumbled upon a little exercise. I call it "Wishes vs. Controls." People have told me that it's literally changed their lives.

Out of sheer desperation and with sweat trickling down my forehead, I reached into my desk, grabbed a pencil and paper, and asked Mom to help me make two lists. The first list I titled "Things I Wish I Could Control." The second list I titled "Things I Really Can Control."

I started naming different things and asking Mom whether they belonged on the "Wishes" list or the "Controls" list. Our results looked something like this:

WISHES

1. The tone of their voices and what they say.
2. Their attitudes.
3. Whether they do their chores.
4. Whether they want to learn and do their homework.
5. The friends they choose.
6. The color of their hair and the parts of their bodies they have pierced.

7. Anything else that involves their muscles and brains instead of mine.

CONTROLS

1. The tone of my voice and my attitude.
2. What I listen to and when I listen to it.
3. Whether I cook what they want to eat.
4. Whether I take them places they want to go.
5. Whether I provide allowance.
6. Which of their possessions I sell to pay for the chores they refuse to complete.
7. When I leave in the morning.

As we finished the lists, Mom's eyes lit up and she said, "I've been trying to control everything that I can't and nothing that I can! The *only* thing I can really control is myself … what I do!" Frankly, I'm glad she figured this out, because I was still lost.

It's amazing what wonderful things other parents have taught me!

Focusing on What You Can Control Is the Key to Success with Children of All Ages!

Though I was a bit slow at the time, did Mom hit the nail on the head? You bet! The only thing we can successfully control is our own behavior, not our kids'!

Sadly, many kids unconsciously pull us into trying to control what we can't. I've known kids who were masters at getting their parents to fight with them over uncontrollable issues, such as their attitudes, nose rings, friends, etc. A parent friend of mine calls this "diversionary warfare."

Sadly, when parents fight battles over issues they can't really control, four very sad things happen:

1. Power struggles take place as the child reasons, "Mom and Dad can't tell me what to do. I'll show them!"

2. Parental energy drains away.
3. Parents have no energy or sanity left over to control what they really can control—their own behavior.
4. The child begins to worry down deep, "If it's so hard for my parents to set limits with me, I must be pretty bad."

How does all of this translate into day-to-day life with strong-willed kids? The answer? *Never tell your kids what to do.* Why? Because that's uncontrollable!

If they decide to fight you, they will always win—and lose in the long run. Instead, focus on what you can control. *Tell them what you are going to do.* Stick to the "Controls" list!

Love and Logic folks speak in what we call enforceable statements. Simply put, when we use enforceable statements, we tell kids what we are going to do instead of what they should.

How does a parent turn things around when things get really nuts and out of control?

Step 1: Make a list of "Wishes" and "Controls."
Step 2: Say to yourself, "Stick to the controllable, stick to the controllable, stick to the controllable."
Step 3: Write an enforceable statement for each issue on the "Controls" list.
Step 4: Experiment with one or two of these statements.

Our mom made a list of "Controls" and "Enforceable Statements." A few are included in the box at the end of this article.

Remember! Love and Logic teaches the importance of genuine compassion and empathy. Enforceable statements won't work if they are delivered with sarcasm or anger.

Mom picked just two of these statements and experimented with them for a week. What happened?

SON: "Mom! When are you gonna wash my clothes? I don't got nothing to wear!"

MOM: (in the sweetest of voices) "I'll be happy to wash your clothes when I feel treated with respect."

SON: "Come on, Mom! I need that stuff."

MOM: "I'll be happy to wash them when I feel respected."

SON: "This is stupid! Why are you being such a pain?"

MOM: "I'll be happy to listen when your voice is calm like mine."

SON: "Fine!" (runs to his room in a huff)

The next day:

SON: "Mom! I need some clothes washed. What am I supposed to do?"

MOM: "I'll be happy to wash them when the yard is cleaned up."

SON: "This is stupid!"

MOM: "I'll listen to you when your voice ..."

SON: (in a sarcastic tone) "Oh. I know! You'll be happy to listen when my voice is calm like yours. Fine!" (runs off in a huff)

Three days later Mom notices her beloved Curtis out in the yard with a rake, cleaning away. An hour later he walks into the kitchen and says something very strange—so strange it sends shivers up and down her spine.

In a soft tone of voice, he says, "Mom, I finished the yard. Will you please wash my clothes?"

Warning! Focusing on the controllable and using enforceable statements may make your kids really mad in the short term. *The good news?* Down deep, kids really need and want their parents to set loving limits.

The ultimate irony of parenthood? Sometimes we really have to make our kids mad in the short term, so they'll have happier lives in the long run.

CONTROLS	ENFORCEABLE STATEMENTS
What I listen to.	*I'll be happy to listen to you when your voice is as calm as mine.*
Whether I cook what they like.	*I'll be happy to cook what you want to eat when I feel treated with respect.*
Whether I take them places they want to go.	*I'll take you the places you want to go when homework and chores are done.*
Whether I provide allowance.	*I'll give allowance when I feel treated with respect.*
Which of their possessions I sell to pay for the chores they refuse to complete.	*If you would rather not do these chores for me, I'll be happy to hire someone to do it, sell one of your things, and pay them with the money.*
When I wash clothes.	*I'll be happy to wash your clothes when I feel treated with respect.*

© 2000 Charles Fay

CLINE'S CORNER

Virtually Every Study Shows That Medication Is Very Helpful in True ADD
By Foster W. Cline, M.D.

VOL. 15, NO. 4

Conclusive studies show that ADD is equally present in boys and girls and that it *generally* does not subside or disappear in adolescence. Often ADD has lifelong effects.

The problem often is harder to detect in girls, because they may be quieter, and ADD without hyperactivity is more common in girls (Offord, D.R.; Faraone, S.Y.; Klein, R.G.; Rieder-Uysal, D.).

All children with ADD need not have continuing issues to face; however, *the most common physical disturbance of college-age young adults* is reported as Attention Deficit Disorder (Shaywitz, S., & Shaywitz, B.).

Studies show that often, the problem does not disappear in adulthood, but continues unabated. It may even be less recognized because the hyperactivity, so common in childhood, gives way in more than half to a more hidden thought fragmentation and difficulty concentrating (McGee, R.; Weiss, G.).

The motor behavior of adults is different than that of children. When children are depressed, or nervous, or anxious, they become *active*. Adults are more likely to become simply more distracted, have difficulty concentrating, and appear preoccupied.

The risk factor of ADD is demonstrated by the fact that 16 percent of those in prison were diagnosed with the problem, while it is generally considered to be present in only 5 percent to 9 percent of the population.

And studies have shown that those with a diagnosis of ADD in childhood have not only an increased chance of incarceration, but an increased level of divorce, an increased participation in risky hobbies and adventures, an increased number of accidents, and an increased number of job failures.

Alcoholism and drug use is higher among those diagnosed in childhood as having ADD. Many of these adults may be "self-medicating," as cocaine and marijuana decrease destructibility (Bellak, L.; Shekim, W.O.; Woolf, A.D.).

Medication of teens and adults, just as with children, often will help with focus and the ability to concentrate, but just as with children, medication will not directly affect attitude, poor self-image, the method of relating to others, personality, and reputation (Klorman, R.; Offord, D.R.; Lir, C.; Rostain, A.L.).

And it is in these areas that Love and Logic excels with principles that help parents and children (and all relationships) show mutual responsibility, mutual respect, and mutual enjoyment.

True ADD is a neurological problem that appears on positron emission tomography as a prefrontal, superior cortex, and corpus striatum problem (Zametkin, A.J.; Sametkin, A.J.; Nordahl, T.E.; Gross, M.). It is *not* simply a behavioral problem.

And just as with any injured organ in the body, the right nutrients and medication may help. Numerous studies show that those with true ADD do best with a combined program of Love and Logic responses *and* medication.

About Medication

The issue of medication often is *needlessly* divisive, for virtually every study shows that medication is very helpful in true ADD. Many parents know that medication helped their correctly diagnosed ADD child "become livable," yet others proclaim, "Medication should never be used." As in all things, the extremes should be avoided.

The bias against medication is as destructive as the bias toward overprescription of it. I will give a couple of examples. I received the following letter from a pediatrician whose own child I had seen one month earlier:

Life is different. I never realized it could be like this with Greg and I don't know how to thank you enough! He and I are having a lot of fun together that would have been impossible before. Frankly, it's like living with an entirely different responsive and thoughtful child!

But, I feel particularly guilty about giving you such a hard time in the office. I want to apologize for that. We had waited many months for an open appointment time "to see the best" and then "the best" interviews us for half an hour, evaluates our child for only twenty minutes, and then recommends the very medication that I have shied away from prescribing in my own practice. I was more than miffed.

I know I can be intimidating, but you brought me up short when you said, "Well, Jack, a few unhappy souls do wait to see 'the best' but then don't take the advice when 'the best' gives it. That's too bad. They shouldn't have waited to see the best. Someone out there would say what they wanted to hear!"

171

In one Canadian city children were denied medication because of local reaction to what was seen as the overuse of medication. These children were treated solely with therapy and good parenting techniques. They were studied over a period of twenty years, into their fourth decade. The unmedicated children were found to have higher rates of school and job failure, delinquency, incarceration, marital failure, and divorce than comparable children who had been treated elsewhere with medication and therapy in a comprehensive plan (Greenfield, B.; Ratey, J.J.).

And there is, contrary to what many of us would think, *no* solid indication that stimulant medication is overused. The fact that stimulant medication for ADD is used so widely is simply a result of its effectiveness with certain children.

Ineffective medication is simply not overused. Alcohol, Ritalin, methamphetamines, sleeping medication, barbiturates, and pain relievers have all, at times, been thought to be overprescribed because they work.

Children who demonstrate hyperactive symptoms—and there are often other associated problems—may be prescribed a variety of medications. It is not useful to go into all of these here, because new medications are constantly being developed, and different clusters of symptoms lead to the use of a variety of medications that your doctor will be glad to explain to you.

But the frontline medications—the ones that are almost always tried first, are the stimulant group of medications. Other medications are frequently and helpfully prescribed. These are different groups of antidepressants, anticonvulsives, and beta blockers.

It is not wise to go into the issues of medication here, as your physician needs to answer your questions about your specific child and his or her needs. Never hesitate to ask your physician:

"What is the medication?"
"Why is it being chosen rather than other medications?"
"What side effects might the medication have?"
"How do I talk to the school about the need for medication?"

"How will you (the physician) follow up with the school and parents concerning the medication's effectiveness?"

Most physicians are very busy, but most want good school and home communication. Often there may be misunderstanding. Many times I have seen cases in which the physician isn't sure that the school wants to be "bothered" and the teacher is fearful of "bothering" the physician and the parent hates to "bother" either, when actually, all of the adults would like to talk to the others!

Because the stimulant medications are so widely prescribed and so often helpful, we will lump the three major medications together and discuss them briefly: methylphenidate (Ritalin), amphetamine (Dexedrine), and a chemically unrelated medication, pemoline (Cylert).

All have similar actions and all have similar side effects. Pemoline acts more slowly, so for diagnostic purposes, when determining if medication is helpful, methylphenidate might be the medication of choice. On the other hand, pemoline is in the blood for thirty-six hours and gives a more even dosage once the diagnosis is established and it is clear that medication is necessary.

Parents usually have some major concerns about these drugs:

• They make the child short (by stopping bone growth).
• They have the potential for addiction.
• The child quits eating.
• The child has trouble sleeping
• The child gets more "hyper."

Let's look at these concerns one at a time.

Short-Kid Concerns
It is true that at one time professionals wondered if Ritalin and its sister drugs had an effect on bone growth, or that the appetite suppression would be so great that adult height would be shortened. Now that concern has been put to rest.

Careful studies have shown that fear of the effect on growth is unwarranted (Liu, C., Robin, A.L.; Brenner, S.). It is true that many of the children who are helped by the stimulants *are* short. But that is correlational with the medication. The medication doesn't cause it.

One foster mom summed up her feelings: "It's a good thing that God keeps these real active ones small!" Many professionals feel that the small size of many very hyperactive children has something to do with their possible neurologic immaturity and the delayed functioning of the pituitary.

Addiction Potential

This can easily be put to rest. As far as I know there is not *one* verified case of a child addicted to Ritalin in the way that most of us envision addiction. Certainly there are many children who when they go off the medication recognize, themselves, that it is necessary for their good functioning.

Presently the literature findings strongly support use of the stimulants in adulthood for those with an ADD diagnosis (Klorman, R., and Brumaghim, J.T.; Wender, P.H.; Shekim, W.O.; Biederjman, J.).

The Child Quits Eating and Sleeping

There is some basis for both of these concerns, for they are side effects of the medication. The stimulants *do* suppress the appetite. And kids do often eat less.

But I have never in all my years of practice seen this happen to the point that the child appears or becomes malnourished to a clinically significant degree. The appetite suppression usually disappears about a month or so into treatment.

The stimulants do keep people awake. In this event, long-lasting pemoline (Cylert) may be helpful in flattening the peaks and valleys of blood level. Parents can best handle their children's sleeping problems with Love and Logic techniques. The child has a bedtime, but not a time when he or she has to go to sleep.

Many parents use naptime for younger children either because they feel the child "needs" a nap or because it gives them a break.

Many children don't need a nap. Many children on Ritalin especially don't need a nap!

However, the moms can very well need a break. So while the mom has a break, the child has "roomtime"—not "naptime." The child can work on a hobby, read a book, listen to the radio or tapes, etc.

Many children now diagnosed with ADD will watch a videotape, which certainly gives parents a break. However, watching videos may be short-term gain for long-term pain. ADD children need to learn task focus. And that is exactly what TV does not teach!

The Child Becomes More "Hyper"

Children become more active on the stimulants for two reasons. Either they are taking too much or they are having an unusual and unexpected reaction to the drug. There are a few children who simply react differently.

So if your child is given Ritalin and becomes even more active, leave the child on the same dose for several days to make sure this is not some artifact that has to do with school or parents' perceptions or whatever. If the hyperactivity continues, other medication may be prescribed.

Medication issues should be discussed in detail with your physician. However, here is some brief information that is generally not in the other works.

Use of Medication

- I have advised those whom I have supervised over the years not to give medication unless their parenting techniques are known to be effective. Ideally, the parents have other great children, and it is Bobby alone that is giving himself and them such great problems.
- If a child is given medication and "maybe it's helping," it's not. Change should be noticeable.

- If the medication isn't making a noticeable change, it should be stopped or the dose adjusted.
- Many children who apparently weren't helped by medication have been, in my practice, undermedicated simply because physicians are so concerned about being accused of overusing stimulant medication that we don't give an adequate dose.
- Never get into a control battle with a child over taking the medication. Parents and teachers always lose this one.

Most children for whom the medication makes a noticeable difference (and only then should it continue to be prescribed) see the difference in their ability to concentrate and want, themselves, to take the medication. One said, "Studying my math problems is so easy. Now I can sit and really think about them."

© 2000 Foster W. Cline, M.D.

Sign up for the *Love and Logic Journal* for yourself, a friend, or your child's teacher.

The *Love and Logic Journal* gives you the positive reinforcement you need.

Our quarterly publication is a great way for parents and teachers to connect with Jim Fay, Charles Fay, Ph.D., and Foster W. Cline, M.D., on a regular basis. In each issue of the *Journal* you will discover the very latest techniques from Jim, Charles, and Foster, presented in an insightful and humorous style. You'll also find exciting articles by guest writers from across the country who are developing creative and innovative ways to use Love and Logic in the home and at school.

Return this order form with your payment TODAY.

Yes! I would enjoy more practical solutions from Jim Fay, Charles Fay, Ph.D., Foster W. Cline, M.D., and other Love and Logic supporters. Please sign me up for a 1-year subscription to the *Love and Logic Journal* at $18. I understand that along with my subscription I may select one free audio valued at $13.95. (Colorado residents, please add 3% [54¢] sales tax to subscription price.)

❏ Check enclosed
❏ Please charge my ❏ VISA ❏ MasterCard ❏ Discover Card

— — — —   — — — —   — — — —   — — — —

Card Expiration Date ____/____ Verification # _____
(found on back of card)
Signature _____

Take advantage of this special BONUS DISCOUNT!

As a *Journal* subscriber you will receive a bonus coupon good for a one-time 10% discount on a variety of Love and Logic books, audios, and videos. You will find this coupon inside the complimentary *Journal* issue you will receive with your free audio. (10% discount excludes package offers, *Becoming a Love and Logic Parent*® program and companion workbooks, *Early Childhood Parenting Made Fun!* program and companion workbooks, *Discipline with Love and Logic* teacher training course, and *9 Essential Skills for the Love and Logic Classroom*® training program and companion workbooks.)

NAME _____

DAYTIME PHONE (_____) _____

ADDRESS _____

CITY _____ STATE _____ ZIP _____

EMAIL ADDRESS _____

Call Customer Service at 800-338-4065 for information on your free audio.